中国世界级非遗文化悦读系列·寻语识遗
丛书主编 魏向清 刘润泽

端午节
（汉英对照）

魏向清 恽如强 主编

Duanwu Festival

南京大学出版社

本书为以下项目的部分成果：

南京大学外国语学院"双一流"学科建设项目

全国科学技术名词审定委员会重点项目"中国世界级非物质文化遗产术语英译及其译名规范化建设研究"

教育部学位中心 2022 年主题案例项目"术语识遗：基于术语多模态翻译的中国非物质文化遗产对外译介与国际传播"

南京大学－江苏省人民政府外事办公室对外话语创新研究基地项目

江苏省社科基金青年项目"江苏世界级非物质文化遗产术语翻译现状与优化策略研究"（19YYC008）

江苏省社科基金青年项目"江苏世界级非遗多模态双语术语库构建研究"（23YYC008）

南京大学暑期社会实践校级特别项目"讲好中国非遗故事"校园文化活动

参与人员名单

丛书主编 魏向清　刘润泽
主　　编 魏向清　恽如强
翻　　译 Alina Gabriela Ariton（佳布丽）
译　　校 Zhujun Shu　Benjamin Zwolinski
学术顾问 宋　颖
出版顾问 何　宁　高　方
中文审读专家（按姓氏拼音首字母排序）
　　　　　　陈　俐　丁芳芳　王笑施
英文审读专家 Colin Mackerras　Leong Liew
参编人员（按姓氏拼音首字母排序）
　　　　　Hannes Bjorn Hafsteinsson（翰思）　何子阳　李洙扬　梁鹏程
　　　　　廖安康　乔丽婷　孙文龙　吴大宁　吴小芳　张心怡
手　　绘 裴梓含（《西塞神舟》之外的全部手绘）　谈嘉瑞（《西塞神舟》）
知识图谱 王朝政
中国历史纪年简表 王朝政
特别鸣谢 江苏省非物质文化遗产保护研究所

编者前言

2019年秋天开启的这次"寻语识遗"之旅,我们师生同行,一路接力,终于抵达了第一个目的地。光阴荏苒,我们的初心、探索与坚持成为这5年奔忙的旅途中很特别,也很美好的回忆。回望这次旅程,所有的困难和克服困难的努力,如今都已经成为沿途最难忘的风景。

这期间,我们经历了前所未有的自主性文化传承的种种磨砺,创作与编译团队的坚韧与执着非同寻常。古人云,"唯其艰难,方显勇毅;唯其磨砺,始得玉成"。现在即将呈现给读者的是汉英双语对照版《中国世界级非遗文化悦读系列·寻语识遗》丛书(共10册)和中文版《中国世界级非遗文化悦读》(1册)。书中汇聚了江苏牵头申报的10项中国世界级非物质文化遗产项目内容,我们首次采用"术语"这一独特的认知线索,以对话体形式讲述中国非遗故事,更活泼生动地去诠释令我们无比自豪的中华非遗文化。

2003年,联合国教科文组织(UNESCO)第32届会议正式通过了《保护非物质文化遗产公约》(以下简称《公约》),人类非物质文化遗产保护与传承进入了全新的历史时期。20多年来,世界"文化多样性"和"人类创造力"得到前所未有的重视和保护。截至2023年12月，中国被列入《人类非物质文化遗产代表作名录》的项目数量位居世界之首（共43项），是名副其实的世界非遗大国。正如《公约》的主旨所述，非物质文化遗产是"文化多样性保护的熔炉，又是可持续发展的保证"，中国非遗文化的世界分享与国际传播将为人类文化多样性注入强大的精神动力和丰富的实践内容。事实上，我国自古就重视非物质文化遗产的保护与传承。"收百世之阙文，采千载之遗韵"，现今留存下来的卷帙浩繁的文化典籍便是记录和传承非物质文化遗产的重要载体。进入21世纪以来，中国政府以"昆曲"申遗为开端，拉开了非遗文化国际传播的大幕，中国非遗保护与传承进入国际化发展新阶段。各级政府部门、学界和业界等多方的积极努力得到了国际社会的高度认可，中国非遗文化正全面走向世界。然而，值得关注的是，虽然目前中国世界级非物质文化遗产的对外译介与国际传播实践非常活跃，但在译介理据与传播模式方面的创新意识有待加强，中国非遗文化的国际"传播力"仍有待进一步提升。

《中国世界级非遗文化悦读系列·寻语识遗》这套汉英双语丛书的编译就是我们为中国非遗文化走向世界所做的一次创新译介努力。该编译项目的缘起是南京大学翻译专业硕士教育中心特色课程"术语翻译"的教学实践与中国文化外译人才培养目标计划。我们秉持"以做促学"和"全过程培养"的教学理念，探索国别化高层次翻译专业人才培养的译者术语翻译能力提升模式，尝试走一条"教、学、研、产"相结合的翻译创新育人之路。从课堂的知识传授、学习，课后的合作研究，到翻译作品的最终产出，我们的教研创新探索结出了第一批果实。

汉英双语对照版丛书《中国世界级非遗文化悦读系列·寻语识遗》被列入江苏省"十四五"时期重点图书出版规划项目，这是对我们编译工作的莫大鼓励和鞭策。与此同时，我们受到来自国际中文教育领域多位专家顾问的启发与鼓励，又将丛书10册书的中文内容合并编成了一个合集《中国世界级非遗文化悦读》，旨在面向国际中文教育的广大师生。2023年夏天，我们这本合集的内容经教育部中外语言交流合作中心教研项目课堂试用，得到了非常积极的反馈。这使我们对将《中国世界级非遗文化悦读》用作非遗文化教材增添了信心。当然，这个中文合集版本也同样适用于国内青少年的非遗文化普及，能让他们在"悦读"过程中感受非遗文化的独特魅力。

汉英双语对照版丛书的编译理念是通过"术语"这一独特认知路径，以对话体形式编写术语故事脚本，带领读者去开启一个个"寻语识遗"的旅程。在每一段旅程中，读者可跟随故事里的主人公，循着非遗知识体系中核心术语的认知线索，去发现、去感受、去学习非遗的基本知识。这样的方式，既保留了非遗的本"真"知识，也彰显了非遗的至"善"取向，更能体现非遗的大"美"有形，是有助于深度理解中国非遗文化的一条新路。为了让读者更好地领会非遗知识之"真善美"，我们将通过二维码链接到"术语与翻译跨学科研究"公众号,计划陆续为所有的故事脚本提供汉语和英语朗读的音频,并附上由翻译硕士专业同学原创的英文短视频内容,逐步完成该丛书配套的多模态翻译传播内容。这其中更值得一提的是,我们已经为这套书配上了师生原创手绘的核心术语插图。这些非常独特的用心制作融入了当代中国青年对于中华优秀传统文化的理解与热爱。这些多模态呈现的内容与活泼的文字一起将术语承载的厚重知识内涵,以更加生动有趣的方式展现在读者面前,以更加"可爱"的方式讲好中国非遗故事。

早在10多年前,全国高校就响应北京大学发起的"非遗进校园"倡议,成立了各类非遗文化社团,并开展了很多有益的活动,初步提升了高校学生非遗文化学习的自觉意识。然而,我们发现,高校学生群体的非遗文化普及活动往往缺乏应有的知识深度,多限于一些浅层的体验性认知,远未达到文化自知的更高要求。我们所做的一项有关端午非遗文化的高校学生群体调研发现,大部分高校学生对于端午民俗的了解较为粗浅,相关非遗知识很是缺乏。试问,如果中国非遗文化不能"传下去",又怎能"走出去"?而且,从根本上来说,没有对自身文化的充分认知,是谈不上文化自信的。"求木之长者,必固其根本;欲流之远者,必浚其泉源。"中国世界级非遗文化的对外译介与国际传播要解决的关键问题是培养国人尤其是青少年的非遗文化自知,形成真正意义上基于文化自知的文化自信,然后才有条件由内而外,加强非遗文化的对外译介与国际传播。非遗文化小书的创新编译过程正是南京大学"非遗进课堂"实践创新的成果,也是南大翻译学子学以致用、培养文化自信的过程。相信他们与老师一起探索与发现,创新与传承,译介与传播的"寻语识遗"之旅定会成为他们求学过程中一个重要的精神印记。

  我们要感谢为这10个非遗项目提供专业支持的非遗研究与实践方面的专家,他们不仅给我们专业知识方面的指导和把关,而且也深深影响和激励着我们,一步一个脚印,探索出一条中国非遗文化"走出去"和"走进去"的译介之路。事实上,这次非常特别的"寻语识遗"之旅,正是因为有了越来越多的同行者而变得更加充满希望。最后,还要特别感谢南京大学外国语学院给了我们重要的出版支持,特别感谢所有参与其中的青年才俊,是他们的创意和智慧赋予了"寻语识遗"之旅始终向前的不竭动力。非遗文化悦读系列是一个开放的非遗译介实践成果系列,愿我们所开辟的这条"以译促知、以译传通"的中国非遗知识世界分享的实践之路上有越来越多的同路人,大家携手,一起为"全球文明倡议"的具体实施贡献更多的智慧与力量。

目 录
Contents

百字说明　A Brief Introduction

内容提要　Synopsis

知识图谱　Key Terms

端午节　Duanwu Festival ······································· 001

屈原　Qu Yuan ··· 011

赛龙舟　Dragon Boat Racing ································· 020

吃粽子　Eating *Zongzi* ·· 029

缠五色丝　Tying Five-Colour Silk Strings ················ 041

打午时水　Fetching Noonday Water ······················· 048

贴午时符　Putting up Noonday Paper Charms ········· 054

画额　Painting Children's Foreheads ······················ 062

斗百草　Matching Herbs ······································ 068

雄黄酒　Realgar Wine ··· 074

避五毒　Warding off Five Poisonous Creatures ········ 082

食五黄　Eating Five Healthy Foods ························ 091

西塞神舟会　The Xisai Sacred Boat Ceremony ········ 100

沐兰汤　Having Herbal Baths ·················115

放纸鸢　Flying Kites ·····························121

佩香囊　Wearing Sachets ·······················130

挂菖蒲　插艾草　Hanging Sweet Flags and Mugwort ·······137

射柳　打马球　Shooting Arrows at Willow Branches and

　　　　Playing Polo ·························149

结束语　Summary ·································167

中国历史纪年简表　A Brief Chronology of Chinese History ········169

百字说明

端午节是中国四大传统节日之一，距今已有2000多年历史。端午节源自上古先民观测天象、形成历法的过程。每逢端午节，人们都会祭祀祈福，希望躲避战乱和疾病，调和阴阳，获得平安与健康。端午文化影响广泛，日本和韩国也有过端午的传统，但其习俗有所变化，呈现出不同的文化特征。2009年，端午节被列入联合国教科文组织的《人类非物质文化遗产代表作名录》。

A Brief Introduction

As one of the four major traditional festivals in China, the Duanwu Festival, also known as the Dragon Boat Festival, has a history of more than 2,000 years. Its origin can be traced back to the calendar created by ancient Chinese people based on their observation of astronomical phenomena. During the festival, people would worship their ancestors and bear their hopes of avoiding wars and illnesses, balancing *yin* and *yang*, and gaining peace and health. The influence of the festival is not confined to China. Some Asian countries such as Japan and Korea celebrate the Duanwu Festival as well, but their customs are different with their own cultural features. In 2009, the Duanwu Festival was inscribed on the Representative List of the Intangible Cultural Heritage of Humanity by UNESCO.

内容提要

端午假期，中国大学生小龙和留学生大卫结伴去湖南汨罗、湖北秭归和黄石游玩，并回到江苏苏州寻找端午的足迹，亲自去体验典型的端午文化。这三省四地是中国端午申遗的代表性地区。在这四个地方，他们不仅体验了饮食、沐浴和娱乐等多方面的端午民俗活动，还参观了博物馆，了解了典型的北方端午民俗，对中国端午文化有了更全面的认识。

Synopsis

During the Duanwu Festival, Xiaolong, a Chinese college student in Suzhou and his friend David, an international student from Britain, went on a trip together. To experience the Duanwu culture, they visited Miluo City in Hunan Province, Zigui County and Huangshi City in Hubei Province, and Suzhou City in Jiangsu Province. These four places across three provinces had been selected to represent the Duanwu festive customs in China's application for the recognition of the Duanwu Festival as an intangible cultural heritage. During the trip, they got to know many different folk customs related to worship rituals, specialties, bathing, entertainment and so forth. In addition, they went to a museum where they learned about the Duanwu practices specific to the northern region and thus developed a better understanding of the Duanwu Festival in China.

知识图谱
Key Terms

- **端午节 / Duanwu Festival**
  - **历史人物 / Historical Figure**
    - 屈原 / Qu Yuan
  - **传统饮食 / Traditional Foods**
    - 吃粽子 / Eating *Zongzi*
    - 食五黄 / Eating Five Healthy Foods
  - **祈愿安康 / Praying for Good Health**
    - 西塞神舟会 / The Xisai Sacred Boat Ceremony
    - 贴午时符 / Pasting Noonday Paper Charms
    - 缠五色丝 / Tying Five-Colour Silk Strings
  - **健身娱乐 / Recreations**
    - 赛龙舟 / Dragon Boat Racing
    - 放纸鸢 / Flying Kites
    - 斗百草 / Matching Herbs
    - 打马球 / Playing Polo
    - 射柳 / Shooting Arrows at Willow Branches
  - **祛病防疫 / Eliminating Diseases and Preventing Epidemics**
    - 画额 / Painting Children's Foreheads
    - 雄黄酒 / Realgar Wine
    - 避五毒 / Warding off Five Poisonous Creatures
    - 沐兰汤 / Having Herbal Baths
    - 佩香囊 / Wearing Sachets
    - 挂菖蒲 / Hanging Sweet Flags
    - 插艾草 / Hanging Mugwort

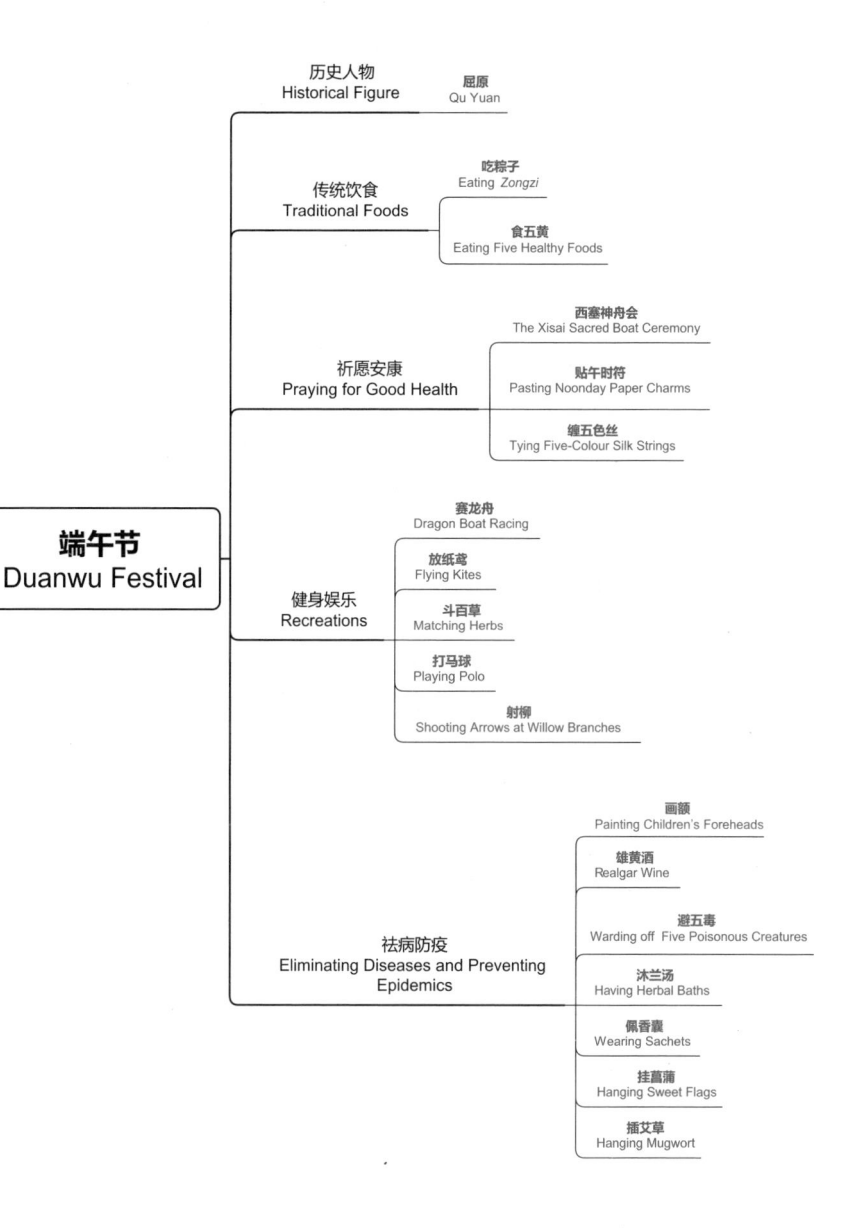

端午节

> 端午节假期将至,大卫提议让小龙陪他一起看龙舟赛,同时也体验一下中国的端午文化。

大　卫:小龙,龙舟节快到了,我想去看龙舟赛。我觉得在中国看龙舟赛应该比在英国看赛艇更有意思。我们找个地方去看看,好不好?

小　龙:好啊。那端午节一放假,我们就去看龙舟赛。

大　卫:端午节?不是龙舟节吗?我们说的是同一个节日吗?

小　龙:你说的龙舟节其实就是我们的端午节。不过,龙舟节的说法虽然在国际上很流行,但并不确切。这样吧,去看龙舟赛之前,我先给你说一说端午文化,怎么样?

大　卫:太好了!快给我讲讲吧。

小　龙：行，我们先说说这个节日的名称。古汉语中，"端"有初始的意思，而"午"和"五"相通，端午就是"初五"，端午节就是农历五月初五的节日。

大　卫：原来是这样。这个节日的英文大多是Dragon Boat Festival，对应的中文就是龙舟节，是因为端午节划龙舟很有名吧？

小　龙：嗯，没错。划龙舟确实是端午节最有影响的传统习俗之一，但并不是端午节的全部习俗哦。除了划龙

端午　Duanwu

舟，端午节还有很多其他重要的习俗呢。

大　卫：是吗？快说说，还有哪些习俗？

小　龙：还有闻雄黄酒，吃粽子，挂菖蒲，插艾草，佩香囊，沐兰汤，打午时水，贴午时符，画额，斗百草，避五毒，食五黄……

大　卫：慢点儿说。这么多习俗，我可真记不住。

小　龙：你只要记住，这些活动都是为了夏季祛病防疫就可以了。这里面还有很多讲究呢。

大　卫：为什么？是因为夏季很容易生病吗？

小　龙：是的。中国有句谚语"端午节，天气热，'五毒'

蝎子　Scorpion　　　　蜈蚣　Centipede

醒，不安宁"，意思是说，农历五月份，天气湿热，毒虫多，是传染病易发的季节。中国古人认为，疾病是邪气导致的，端午节很多活动都是为了除邪气、保健康。可以这么说，端午节是中国古人的"卫生防疫节"。

大 卫：可我一直听说，划龙舟是为了纪念中国古代大诗人屈原，是吗？

小 龙：那是端午节的传说之一。相传划龙舟和吃粽子是为了纪念投江的屈原。事实上，早在屈原之前就有端午节，各地很早就形成了端午除病防疫的习俗。

大 卫：嗯，听起来很有意思。那我们就去体验一下吧。

小 龙：好，我们来个端午四地游，怎么样？

大 卫：为什么要去四个地方呢？

小 龙：前两天我刚查了资料，了解中国哪些地方的端午习俗保留得比较好。湖南汨罗、湖北秭归和黄石，还有我们江苏苏州，这四个地方的端午习俗最有代表性。端午节被列入联合国教科文组织的《人类非物质文化遗产代表作名录》，就是以这四个地方的端午习俗为典型申报成功的。你说要不要去这些地方呢？

大　卫：嗯，有道理，这四个地方我们都要去。
小　龙：那我们先去湖南和湖北的三个地方，回来之后，我们再专门去体验苏州的端午习俗。
大　卫：好，我们来个三省四地的端午游。

Duanwu Festival

The Duanwu Festival was around the corner. David suggested to Xiaolong that they go to watch the dragon boat racing and experience the culture of China's Duanwu Festival.

David: Xiaolong, the Dragon Boat Festival is coming up. I'd like to watch a dragon boat race. It must be more interesting than the rowing competition in the UK. Let's pick a place to watch it, shall we?

Xiaolong: Sure. We'll go to watch the dragon boat racing as soon as the Duanwu Festival holiday begins.

David: Duanwu Festival? Isn't it the Dragon Boat Festival? Are we talking about the same thing?

Xiaolong: What you call the Dragon Boat Festival is in fact the Duanwu Festival we celebrate in China. Even though the name Dragon Boat Festival is widely used abroad, it isn't entirely accurate. Let me introduce you a few things about the Duanwu culture before we go to the dragon boat racing.

David: That's great! I can't wait to hear more about it.

Xiaolong: OK, let's start with its name. In classical Chinese, *duan* (端) means beginning, and the pronunciation of *wu* (午) is similar to that of *wu* (五), and both of them can mean "five". So, they are interchangeable. In short, it's a festival occurring on the fifth day of the fifth lunar month in China.

David: Oh, I see! This festival is often called "the Dragon Boat Festival" in English. Maybe it's so named because the dragon boat racing is a well-known activity on that day.

Xiaolong: You're right. The dragon boat racing is indeed one of the most famous traditional practices of the Duanwu Festival, but not the only one on that day. There're other important customs.

David: Really? Like what?

Xiaolong: Like sniffing realgar wine, eating *zongzi* (粽子), hanging sweet flags and mugwort, wearing sachets, having herbal baths, fetching noonday water, pasting noonday paper charms, painting children's foreheads, matching herbs, warding off five poisonous creatures, eating five healthy foods…

David: Wait a minute. Slow down, please. I couldn't remember so many customs.

Xiaolong: Well, there's a lot to say about each of them, but you only have to bear in mind that these activities are all done for the purpose of eliminating diseases and preventing epidemics in summer.

David: Why? Is it easy to get sick in summer?

Xiaolong: Yes, indeed. There's an old saying in Chinese : "When the Duanwu Festival comes and the weather is hot, the five poisons are awake, no peace to stay." This means that in the fifth lunar month when it's hot and humid, many poisonous creatures are lurking around, and then infectious diseases are most likely to spread. In ancient China, people believed diseases were brought about by evil *qi* (气). Many of the activities organized during the Duanwu Festival are meant to ward off evil *qi* and protect people. Actually, one could say that it was a festival of epidemic prevention in ancient China.

David: But I heard that the purpose of the dragon boat racing is to commemorate Qu Yuan, a prominent Chinese poet. Am I right?

Xiaolong: Well, you're quite right. But there're many versions in terms of the origin of the festival. Qu Yuan is just one of them. The legend goes that people adopted the customs to row dragon boats and eat *zongzi* to commemorate Qu Yuan who drowned himself in the Miluo River. In fact, people had celebrated the Duanwu Festival long before Qu Yuan died. Back then, the customs of the festival were practiced across the country with the purpose of preventing diseases and epidemics in the summertime.

David: Oh, sounds interesting. Why not go and see by ourselves then?

Xiaolong: Good idea. What about a trip to four different places during the Duanwu Festival?

David: Why four places?

Xiaolong: Honestly, I found out only a few days ago places where Duanwu traditions have been better preserved. To be specific, Miluo City in Hunan Province, Zigui County and Huangshi City in Hubei Province, as well as Suzhou in Jiangsu Province are considered the most representative places for preserving the customs of the Duanwu Festival. The local customs in these places were in fact recorded in China's proposal for the inclusion of the Duanwu Festival in UNESCO's Representative List of the Intangible Cultural Heritage of Humanity in 2009. So, don't you think we should go to visit these places?

David: Well, sounds reasonable. We should go to all these four places.

Xiaolong: OK, we'll go to the other three places first and then take a look at the Duanwu customs here in Suzhou when we get back.

David: I'm really looking forward to this trip.

屈原

> 端午假期第一天,小龙和大卫来到了他们文化体验之旅的第一站——湖南汨罗。

大　卫:汨罗江真美啊!

小　龙:是啊,可这是大诗人屈原投江自尽的地方。

大　卫:他为什么要投江呢?

小　龙:说来话长。屈原生于公元前约340年,是战国时期楚国人。当时,有二十多个诸侯国各自为政,比较大的是齐、楚、燕、韩、赵、魏、秦七国。秦国总想吞并其他六国,称霸天下。

大　卫:嗯,中文课上老师讲过"战国七雄"的故事,那时战乱很频繁。

小　龙:是的。屈原是楚国大夫,主张改革楚国政治,联合其他五国共同抵抗秦国。楚王不但没有采纳他的主张，反而把他赶出了国都。屈原离开后，依然关心自己国家的命运。当他听到楚国国都被秦国占领的消息时，悲痛万分，决意以身殉国，投汨罗江自尽。

大　卫：原来是这样。看来屈原不仅是个大诗人，还是个爱国者。可他和端午节有什么关系呢？

小　龙：有啊。据说，屈原是在五月初五投的江。得知消息后，当地老百姓纷纷划船去营救他，但没能救上来。当地人为了纪念他，每年这一天都会祭拜屈

屈原　Qu Yuan

原,举行龙舟赛。

大　卫:所以,划龙舟就是为了纪念屈原,对吧?

小　龙:不完全对。其实划龙舟这个民俗活动早在屈原之前就已经存在了。关于它的起源有不同说法。不过可以肯定的是,这个活动与古代祭祀和龙图腾崇拜有关系。

大　卫:哦,是这样啊。

小　龙:是的。根据传说,还有一个端午习俗也和屈原有关。

大　卫:什么习俗呢?

小　龙:吃粽子。粽子是用粽叶包裹糯米煮熟后吃的一种食物。大卫,你吃过吗?

大　卫:还没有。好吃吗?有机会要尝一尝,你先跟我说说那个传说吧。

小　龙:好的。相传屈原死后,汨罗的百姓就把大米扔进江里去喂鱼虾,想让鱼虾吃饱,就不会再去吃屈原的尸首。后来,屈原托梦给百姓,说江里有条蛟龙把大米吃完了。他让人们用箬竹叶和五色线把米包裹起来再投入江中,因为蛟龙害怕箬竹叶和五色线。

大　卫:看来端午节和屈原的关系真的很密切。

小　龙：确实，后来人们将端午节与屈原投江的传说联系起来，主要是为了纪念这位忧国忧民的大诗人。

大　卫：明白了。听说屈原写过很多著名作品，主要有哪些呢？

小　龙：屈原的代表作是《离骚》《天问》《九歌》。对了，2020年中国首次执行火星探测任务的探测器"天问一号"，就是以屈原的诗歌《天问》命名的。

大　卫："天问"是什么意思呢？

小　龙：简单地说，"天问"就是询问上天的意思。在《天问》里，屈原对天地、自然和人世等一切事物大胆发问，体现了追求真理和勇于探索的精神。中国航天探测器用"天问一号"命名，表示中国开启了问天之旅、宇宙之行。

大　卫：这个名字很有意义，也很有气魄。

> 这时远处传来阵阵锣鼓声。

小　龙：大卫你听，好像有锣鼓声。应该是龙舟赛开始了。

大　卫：我们赶紧去看看吧。

Qu Yuan

> On the first day of the Duanwu holiday, Xiaolong and David arrived at Miluo City in Hunan Province. It was the first stop of their trip, where their journey of experiencing the Duanwu culture began.

David: The Miluo River is really beautiful!

Xiaolong: Yes, it is. But unfortunately, the famous poet Qu Yuan drowned himself in this very river.

David: Why did he do so?

Xiaolong: Well, it's a long story. Qu Yuan was born around 340 BC and lived in the State of Chu. At that time, there were more than twenty independent states. Among them, Qi, Chu, Yan, Han, Zhao, Wei and Qin were comparatively powerful. Qin had always been trying to annex the other six states.

David: Ah, my Chinese teacher once told us the story of "the Seven Powers of the Warring States Period". It was a time of incessant warfare.

Xiaolong: Exactly. Qu Yuan was a state official of Chu. He advocated for reforming Chu's political system and allying with the other five states to resist Qin's threat of military invasion, but unfortunately his ideas were rejected. Not only did the king of Chu disregard his political advice, but also banished him from the capital. But even after his departure, Qu Yuan was still preoccupied with the fate of Chu. Later, he extremely grieved at hearing that the capital had eventually been occupied by Qin. So, he jumped into the Miluo River, and determined to die together with his state.

David: I see. So, Qu Yuan is not only a great poet but also a statesman who loves his state to the extent of dying for it. But does he have anything to do with the Duanwu Festival?

Xiaolong: Of course. He's said to have drowned himself in the river on the fifth day of the fifth lunar month. Upon hearing it, people rushed out with their boats to rescue him, but failed. From then on, on this day of every year, the locals would honour Qu Yuan by organising dragon boat races.

David: So, the purpose of the dragon boat racing is to commemorate Qu Yuan, right?

Xiaolong: Not exactly. As a matter of fact, the dragon boat racing as a custom had existed long before his time. Even though there're different versions about its origin, this activity is most certainly connected to ancient rituals and dragon worships.

David: Oh, got it.

Xiaolong: According to legend, there's another custom related to Qu Yuan.

David: What's it?

Xiaolong: Eating *zongzi*. *Zongzi* in Chinese is a type of food made of glutinous rice wrapped in reed leaves and then boiled. David, have you ever tried it?

David: Not yet. Does it taste good? I'll give it a try when I get the chance. Could you please tell me more about that legend?

Xiaolong: Sure. It's said that after Qu Yuan's death, the local people of Miluo threw rice into the river to feed the fish and other aquatic animals so that they wouldn't eat Qu Yuan's body. Later, the poet appeared in the locals' dreams, telling them that a dragon in the river had eaten all the rice. He told them to wrap the rice in reed leaves and tie them with five-colour threads because the dragon was afraid of the two things.

David: It seems the connection between the festival and Qu Yuan is very strong.

Xiaolong: That's true. Later, people associated the festival with the legend of Qu Yuan drowning himself in the river. In so doing, people paid homage to the great poet who had always been concerned for his country and people.

David: Understood. And I know Qu Yuan wrote many famous poems. What're his masterpieces?

Xiaolong: His masterpieces include *Lisao*, *Tianwen* and *The Nine Songs*. By the way, the spacecraft for China's first Mars exploration mission in 2020 was named Tianwen-1. It used Tianwen, the very title of one of Qu Yuan's poems.

David: What does it mean?

Xiaolong: Simply put, it means literally "asking heaven". In *Tianwen*, Qu Yuan poses a series of questions about everything in life: the heaven and earth, the nature and the human world. It reflects his quest for truth and his inquisitive spirit. To name the Chinese spacecraft Tianwen-1 suggests that China has embarked on its journey to explore the universe.

David: Wow, it's truly a meaningful and compelling name.

> Rolls of drums can be heard from afar.

Xiaolong: David, listen! Do you hear the drums? The dragon boat racing must have started.

David: Come on. Let's hurry.

赛龙舟

> 小龙和大卫快步来到了江边。在龙舟节活动现场的服务台前,小龙领到一本有关龙舟节的宣传册。

大　卫:小龙,这里是不是可以说"人山人海"呀?

小　龙:对啊,大卫,你用词很恰当。今天是汨罗龙舟节。大卫,你瞧,宣传册上说划龙舟起源于古代南方的送瘟神仪式。

大　卫:送瘟神?瘟神是什么?

小　龙:瘟神就是传说中掌管瘟疫的恶神,据说能散播疫情或停止疫情。端午节前后,南方天气湿热,疾病容易传播,所以古人把象征瘟神的神偶用船送走。等我们去湖北,会专门去看送百毒的神舟。百毒就是很多种对人有害的毒物和疾病。

大　卫:送瘟神就是送走瘟疫、祈求平安的意思吧?

划龙舟　Dragon Boat Racing

小　龙：没错。当然，后来又加上了纪念屈原的另一层意思。但不管怎么说，现在龙舟赛已经成为一项竞技娱乐活动了。南方很多地方端午节都要举办龙舟赛。

大　卫：龙舟赛不仅中国有，国际上都很流行呢。我明白了，难怪西方人会用"龙舟节"这个词来指端午节呢。

小　龙：中国民间非常看重赛龙舟、夺锦标。有的地方甚至有"宁愿荒废一年田，不愿输掉一年船"的说法。走，我们到前面去看看。你瞧，船上装饰了龙头和龙尾，很像水里的游龙吧。

大　卫：嗯。龙舟身上的彩绘也很漂亮。每条龙舟上的人不少呢，少说也有20人。看那个鼓手敲得多起劲。这就像剑桥、牛津的赛艇对抗赛一样，但更热闹、更好看。

小　龙：你观察得还挺仔细呢。实际上，龙舟运动早就推广到世界各地了，欧洲不少国家和大学都有龙舟队参加国际赛事。龙舟上的人比赛艇上的人多很多，所以控制起来更困难，需要紧密配合、反复练习。

大　卫：龙舟上这么多人，他们是怎么分工的呢？

小　龙：龙舟上的人分划手、舵手和鼓手。那个鼓手非常重要，待会儿你仔细观察一下。

现场发令枪响起，龙舟赛开始了。

大　卫：敲鼓不就是给划龙舟的人加油鼓劲吗？难道还有其他作用？

小　　龙：看一会儿你就知道鼓手的重要了。

大　　卫：哇，划得好快呀。你看，他们动作多整齐呀。哦，我看明白了，鼓手是在用鼓点指挥大家，协调节奏。

小　　龙：对啊。鼓手和舵手都非常重要，一个指挥划舟，一个掌握方向。划龙舟靠的就是团队协作。龙舟队里，划手人数多，作用大。如果划手动作不整齐，肯定划不快。

大　　卫：那平时他们一定得多训练，相互配合好。

小　　龙：那当然了。鼓手通过鼓点调节划桨节奏。一旦节奏乱了，不仅划得慢，还会浪费划手体力。舵手在船尾，掌控龙舟方向，不然划手和鼓手的努力就白费了。你看那条划在最前面的龙舟，队员们动作多整齐呀。

> 两人兴致勃勃地看完了整场比赛。

大　　卫：这么快就结束了，我还没看够呢。

小　　龙：没关系，这里好玩的事儿多着呢。

大　　卫：那我们现在去哪里呢？

小　　龙：我们去吃粽子吧。

Dragon Boat Racing

> Xiaolong and David made their way to the riverside quickly. Xiaolong picked up a brochure on the Duanwu Festival at the information desk.

David: What a crowd! Can I say this place is *renshan renhai* (人山人海), Xiaolong?

Xiaolong: Exactly! You just used that Chinese idiom correctly. The dragon boat racing is held today to celebrate the festival. Take a look at this brochure. It says the custom of rowing dragon boats originated from the ceremony of expelling the god of plagues in ancient southern China.

David: Expelling the god of plagues? Who's he?

Xiaolong: According to legend, it's an evil god that can start and stop the spread of diseases. In southern China, the weather is usually hot and humid in the early fifth lunar month, just the perfect conditions for diseases to spread. So, people in ancient times would place this god's figurine on a boat and send it far away. We'll see the Sacred Dragon Boat warding off all poisons harmful to people when we go to Hubei.

David: So, people chased away this wicked god to stay safe and healthy. Am I right?

Xiaolong: Yes, indeed. Later, rowing dragon boats was also linked to the commemoration of Qu Yuan. Anyway, now it has become a much-loved competition and entertainment. Dragon boat races are organized in many places in southern China during the Duanwu Festival.

David: So far as I know, dragon boat races are popular not only in China, but also internationally. Now I see why westerners use the expression "Dragon Boat Festival" to refer to the Duanwu Festival.

Xiaolong: In China, people take the race very seriously. It's said that people would rather leave farmlands unattended for a year than lose an annual dragon boat competition! Come on! Let's go to the front. Look! The boats are decorated with dragon heads and tails. Don't they look like swimming dragons in the river?

David: Surely, they do. And they're all nicely painted. There're quite a few people on each boat, twenty at least, I'd say. Look at that drummer. He's playing with such vigour! It's just like the Boat Race between Oxford and Cambridge, but more exciting to watch.

Xiaolong: You certainly have an eye for details. In fact, the dragon boat racing has been promoted all over the world. Many European countries and universities have dragon boat teams to participate in international competitions. It's not easy to row a dragon boat because there're far more crew members on it than on a racing shell. They need to cooperate closely and practice more.

David: There are so many people on a dragon boat. How do they divide the labour?

Xiaolong: The crew members on each boat consist of paddlers, a steersman, and a drummer. The drummer is very important. Take a good look at him after the race begins.

> At the sound of the starting gun, the race was kicked off.

David: The drum is beaten to cheer the rowers on, isn't it? What else can it do?

Xiaolong: Just keep watching and you'll understand why the drummer is so important.

David: Wow! They're so fast! Just look at how well the paddlers coordinate their strokes. Oh, I get it. The drummer instructs the crew by the rhythmic beating of his drum and keeps their strokes at the same rate.

Xiaolong: Exactly. Both the drummer and the steersman are integral to the team. One passes on commands, and the other controls the direction. The majority of the crew members are paddlers. If they're not rowing at the same rate, it'll be impossible for the boat to move very fast. You see, teamwork is everything in the dragon boat racing.

David: I guess they must train hard to build up good teamwork.

Xiaolong: Absolutely. As I've mentioned before, the drummer regulates the strokes through his drumbeats. If he doesn't keep the paddlers in sync, not only will the boat slow down, the paddlers would also run out of their energy soon. At the same time, the steersman at the stern makes sure the boat goes in a straight line. Otherwise, the efforts of other members will go down the drain. Look at the leading dragon boat. They are rowing with such a perfect rhythm.

Xiaolong and David watched the entire contest with great interest.

David: Ooh, is it over already? I want to watch more.

Xiaolong: No worries. There are a lot more fun to come around here.

David: So, what's next?

Xiaolong: Let's go to eat some *zongzi*.

吃粽子

> 看完赛龙舟，小龙带着大卫去小吃店品尝粽子。

大　卫：小龙，端午节吃粽子也有什么故事吧？

小　龙：倒不是故事，是科学道理。端午节吃粽子的习俗源于古代夏至①。古人认为，夏至当天，阳气最旺。如果饮食不当，人就很容易上火，对身体不好。

大　卫："上火"是什么意思？

小　龙："上火"是民间说法，又称"热气"。按照中医理论，上火是人体阴阳失衡后出现的一种症状。

大　卫：怎么能看出来上火呢？

小　龙：上火有很多症状，比如，眼睛红肿、口角糜烂、牙痛、咽喉痛等。这时候就要注意饮食调理了。

大　卫：那吃粽子和上火有什么关系呢？

小　龙：古时候人们用黄米包粽子。黄米营养丰富，但性温

粽子 Zongzi

热，属阳，多吃了会上火。人们就想到用箬竹叶来包裹黄米。箬竹性寒凉，属阴，用它的叶子包裹黄米，是以阴裹阳，阴阳中和，就不容易上火了。尤其是端午时节，天气转热，古人认为这样吃，既能品美味，又能保健康。是不是很科学？

大 卫：嗯，确实挺有道理。看来，在中国，"阴阳"无处不在呀。吃个粽子也讲究阴阳平衡。那我们也来吃个粽子吧。

小　龙：大卫你看，师傅们正在现场包粽子呢。

大　卫：动作真快！我还没看明白，就包好了。

小　龙：听说包粽子也有窍门，就是"一卷一盖一扎"。你看，师傅双手将粽叶卷成漏斗形，往里面放入糯米和馅料，然后用上部多出的粽叶盖住漏斗口，再翻转粽叶，包裹紧，最后用五色线捆绑好。

大　卫：粽子里除了放糯米，还要放馅料？像包饺子一样有各种口味吧？我要看看哪种我最爱吃。

小　龙：说起馅料，那可就多啦。其实粽子通常是以馅料命名的，比如鲜肉粽、豆沙粽、栗子粽、红枣粽，有的甜有的咸。

大　卫：听上去都不错呀。我想每一种都尝尝。

小　龙：那可不行。粽子虽好吃，也不能多吃。

大　卫：为什么？

小　龙：因为粽子里面的糯米很黏，吃多了不容易消化。

大　卫：好的，那就吃一个，品尝一下。

小　龙：大卫，你知道吗？粽子不仅好吃，还有很多好的寓意呢。首先，因为"粽"与祖宗的"宗"谐音，所以端午节吃粽子有希望光宗耀祖的意思。

大　卫：光宗耀祖是什么意思呢？

小　龙：光宗耀祖就是子孙后代做得好，可以让祖先和家族骄傲。中国文化的特点之一就是祖先崇拜，端午吃粽子也是祈求家族兴旺。

大　卫：嗯，我注意到了。之前在南方旅游时，我看到过很多家族祠堂。

小　龙：是的，过去中国人喜欢一个家族住在同一个地方，规模大一点的家族都有自己的祠堂，同族人供奉同一个祖先。

大　卫：我们英国人也讲究血缘血统，尤其是皇室贵族。

小　龙：中国文化中还有个很特别的现象，那就是喜欢用谐音字表达各种寓意。

大　卫：谐音字对我来说有点儿难。问个小问题，谐音字只表达好事吗？

小　龙：不一定，好事坏事都有。这个问题比较复杂，以后找时间专门给你讲吧。我们先说说和粽子有关的谐音字吧。粽子的包法不同，表达的寓意不一样，比如九子粽，就是将九只粽子包裹好，连成一串，大的在上，小的在下，用九种不同颜色的丝线串起来。

大　卫：为什么要九只粽子连成一串呢？

小　龙：在汉语里，"九"除了表示实在的数字，也指多的意思。送九子粽是祝福新婚夫妇多生孩子，人丁兴旺。

大　卫：嗯，让我想想。"粽子"与"中子"谐音，表示求子。九表示多，九子粽就是很多孩子的意思。中国文化的表达习惯真有意思。

小　龙：还有，"枣粽"与"早中"发音也相似。在古代南方，读书人参加科举考试②，当天早晨一定要吃枣馅的粽子，意思是期望早日考中。这个习俗延续至今，很多南方人考试前还会专门吃枣粽。

大　卫：嗯，这个我记住了。以后考试前，我也要吃个枣粽，保佑我考试顺利通过。

注释：
① 夏至：中国二十四节气中的第十个节气，在每年公历6月21日或22日。各地夏至风俗不同，有的地方吃面，有的地方吃粽子。
② 科举考试：科举是古代中国通过考试选拔官吏的制度。

Eating *Zongzi*

> Once the race was over, Xiaolong and David went to a restaurant to eat *zongzi*.

David: Xiaolong, why do Chinese people eat *zongzi* on the Duanwu Festival? What's the story behind it?

Xiaolong: Well, this custom is based on a theory rather than a story. It originated from the summer solstice[1] in ancient times. People believed that *yang qi* (阳气), or the heat was at its most potent during the summer solstice, and they would suffer from overheating if they didn't eat properly.

David: What do you mean by overheating?

Xiaolong: It's a folk concept that suggests the body is in a state of excessive heat, a consequence of the imbalance between the *yin* and *yang* in one's body.

David: How do you know when it strikes?

Xiaolong: Well, the symptoms include red and swollen eyes, perleche, toothache, sore throat and so on. Once these signs show, you should be careful of your diet.

David: What do these signs have to do with eating *zongzi*?

Xiaolong: In the past, people made *zongzi* with millet. Nutritious as it is, millet is a warming or *yang* food, which is hot-natured. It would cause overheating if you eat too much. So, ancient people came up with a solution. They wrapped the millet with reed leaves, which are cold or *yin* in nature. It's believed that the reed leaves could balance the hot nature of millet, and thus overheating is less likely to happen. It's thought that *zongzi* made this way not only tastes delicious, but also does good to our health. What do you think of it? Isn't it very smart?

David: Yes, it does make sense. Chinese people seem to think of everything in terms of *yin* and *yang*. Even when you eat *zongzi*, you consider how to balance them. Well, let's get some, too.

Xiaolong: Sure. David, look! They are making *zongzi* there.

David: They're working so fast. I can barely see how they make them.

Xiaolong: Actually, it's not difficult to make them if you follow three steps. Look at them. First, fold the leaf into a cone shape to contain glutinous rice and different fillings. Then, fold the excess leaf downward to seal the cone. Finally, wrap it tightly with five-colour threads.

David: Different fillings? I assume then *zongzi* must come in all sorts of flavours, just like Chinese dumplings, right? I'd like to see which is my favourite.

Xiaolong: There's a variety of fillings and the name tells what's inside, such as pork *zongzi*, bean paste *zongzi*, chestnut *zongzi* and red jujube *zongzi*. There're sweet and savoury options.

David: My mouth is already watering. I want to give them all a try.

Xiaolong: That's probably not a good idea. *Zongzi* is tasty, but you can't eat too much at a time.

David: How so?

Xiaolong: Because the glutinous rice is sticky and uneasy to digest.

David: Alright, I'll try one then.

Xiaolong: You know what? *Zongzi* isn't just a delicacy. There're some interesting sayings about eating *zongzi* during the Duanwu Festival. First, it has the implication of bringing honour to one's ancestors. That's because the pronunciation of the character *zong* (粽) in *zongzi* (粽子) is similar to that of the character *zong* (宗) in *zuzong* (祖宗), which means an ancestor.

David: I don't quite understand.

Xiaolong: Well, "to bring honour to one's ancestors" means that the younger generations can bring a good name to their ancestors and families by succeeding in their life and work. The ancestor worship is an important part of our culture and eating *zongzi* is linked to it. It represents a way to pray for the prosperity of one's family.

David: Yes, I noticed. I saw many ancestral halls during my trips in southern China.

Xiaolong: You're right. In the past, people from the same clan preferred to live together. Larger families had their own ancestral halls, where they worshipped their ancestors.

David: It reminds me of the history and lineage of the British royal family.

Xiaolong: Besides, Chinese people like to express various implications with words that have the same or similar pronunciation. It's a typical Chinese way to play with words.

David: But Chinese puns are a bit over my head. I have a quick question. Are the puns always used for positive things?

Xiaolong: Not necessarily. They can be positive or negative. This subject is rather complicated. We'll dive into it another time. Now, let's focus on some puns related to *zongzi*. Depending on the ways it's wrapped, *zongzi* may carry different implications. For example, *jiuzi zong*（九子粽）refers to nine *zongzi* which are of varying sizes and shapes and fastened by silk threads of nine different colours, with the bigger ones on top and smaller ones at the bottom.

David: Why do they tie nine *zongzi* together?

Xiaolong: In Chinese, *jiu* or nine expresses the idea of "many" rather than an exact quantity in this case. So, people make this string of *zongzi* to wish newly-wed couples to have a growing family with many children.

David: Now, let me see. In Chinese, the pronunciation of *zongzi* is similar to that of *zhongzi* (中子), which means to be blessed with a child, and *jiu* means many. They together mean to be blessed with many children. How interesting it is!

Xiaolong: Yes, indeed. Oh, I remembered another one. The pronunciations of *zaozong* (枣粽, jujube *zongzi*) and *zaozhong* (早中, passing exams sooner) are almost the same in Chinese. In some southern places of ancient China, scholars ate *zongzi* with jujube fillings in the morning before taking the imperial examination[2]. They believed this would help them pass the exam on their first try. The practice continues to this day in the south of China, where people like to eat jujube *zongzi* before taking exams.

David: OK, I'll keep this in mind. I'll have jujube *zongzi* before tests. I really hope it can help me pass all exams with high grades.

Notes:

1. **Summer solstice**: The tenth of the 24 Chinese solar terms. It occurs on June 21st or 22nd in the Gregorian calendar. The summer solstice is celebrated in different ways across the country. For example, people eat noodles in some places, and *zongzi* in others.

2. **Imperial examination**: It's a system for selecting officials through examinations in ancient China.

缠五色丝

> 吃完粽子,小龙和大卫继续在汨罗观光。

大　卫:小龙,你看,那些小孩手腕上缠着彩线手环,真好看。

小　龙:哦,那叫缠五色丝,也是一种端午习俗。过去端午

缠五色丝　Tying Five-Colour Silk Strings

节清晨，各家大人起床后的第一件事，就是在孩子手腕、脚腕、脖子上缠五色丝。

大　卫：为什么要用五色的丝呢？

小　龙：中国古代崇尚红、黄、蓝、白、黑五色，认为五色是吉祥色，把五种颜色的线拧在一起，系在身上，就能辟邪防病。古代五色丝也叫长命缕、辟兵缯。

大　卫：长命缕？辟兵缯？

小　龙：是的，古汉语中"缕"是"线"的意思，"缯"指的是丝织品。据说，在2200多年前的汉朝时就有缠五色丝的习俗。人们把五种颜色的丝线拧成彩缕，缠在手臂或脖子上，辟邪防病，尤其会给孩子缠在手腕上，保佑他们不被兵器、鬼怪伤害，也保佑他们远离瘟疫。

大　卫：原来是这样。我以为是为了漂亮，就像戴手镯一样，没想到这还是端午习俗。

小　龙：过去五色丝不可以随意摘下或丢弃，只能在夏季第一场大雨或第一次洗澡后抛到河里，让河水把瘟疫、疾病带走，这样才可以保佑小孩子安康。后来五色丝发展成各种漂亮、好玩的香囊。等回苏州，我们专门去找端午香囊。

大　卫：好啊。那五色丝是用什么线做的？对材料有特别要求吗？

小　龙：材料倒是没什么特别的要求，丝线、棉线都行，不过五种颜色是有讲究的。

大　卫：不就是红、黄、蓝、白、黑五种颜色吗？

小　龙：这五色可不一般。它们代表着金、木、水、火、土五种性质的事物。中国古人把宇宙万物划分为金、木、水、火、土性质的五大类，认为它们的运动变化构成世间的一切物质。五色丝的颜色分别代表这五大类物质：白色代表金，蓝色代表木，黑色代表水，红色代表火，黄色代表土。

大　卫：明白了。五色丝除了用来缠手腕和扎粽子，还有什么作用？

小　龙：五色丝还可以用来编织小网兜。端午节人们会在五彩网兜里装上煮熟的鸡蛋或鸭蛋，挂在孩子脖子上，寓意也是保平安健康。

大　卫：那好，等会儿我们也买五色丝缠手腕上，保佑我们旅行平安，身体健康。

小　龙：学得很快嘛。走，说买就买。

Tying Five-Colour Silk Strings

> After they finished eating *zongzi*, Xiaolong and David continued looking around Miluo City.

David: Xiaolong, look! Those kids are wearing coloured string bracelets on their wrists. How nice they are.

Xiaolong: Oh, they're five-colour silk strings. Actually, that's another Duanwu Festival custom. In the past, the very first thing parents would do on the morning of the festival was to tie those strings around children's wrists, ankles, and necks.

David: Why five colours?

Xiaolong: People believed that red, yellow, blue, white, and black were auspicious colours. They thought that twisting threads of those colours together and wearing them would provide protection against evils and diseases. That's why it was also called the string of longevity and the silk of safety respectively.

David: The string of longevity and the silk of safety?

Xiaolong: Exactly. They say this custom dates back to more than 2,200 years ago, the Han Dynasty when people would twist a string with threads of five colours and tie it to their arms or necks to help them ward off evil *qi* and diseases. They would especially tie the string on kids' wrists so as to protect them from the harm of weapons, ghosts, and plagues.

David: I see. I thought it was only an accessory, just like usual bracelets. I didn't know it was a Duanwu tradition.

Xiaolong: People weren't allowed to take it off or dispose of it as they liked. Only after a heavy rain or taking the first bath in the summer could they throw it into a river to let the water wash away all diseases. In this way children who wore the strings would be protected. Later, five-colour silk strings were used for making all sorts of pretty and interesting sachets. We'll see

Duanwu sachets when we go back to Suzhou.

David: Great. Is the string made of any special materials?

Xiaolong: Not really. Either silk or cotton would work, but the colours can't be chosen at random.

David: Red, yellow, blue, white, and black, right?

Xiaolong: Yes. They're specially selected colours to represent substances of five different properties, namely Metal, Wood, Water, Fire, and Earth. Ancient Chinese people categorized the whole universe into these five major substances. Substances of these five categories were in motion and ever-changing, making up everything in the world. The five colours of the string correspond to the five categories of substances: white stands for Metal, blue for Wood, black for Water, red for Fire, and yellow for Earth.

David: This well explains the custom. Then, besides bracelets and *zongzi*, what else can five-colour silk strings be used for?

Xiaolong: Well, you can also weave a tiny net bag with them. During the Duanwu Festival, people would put a boiled egg into a tiny net bag and hang it around children's necks to keep them safe and healthy.

David: Such fun. We can also buy some five-colour silk strings to wear on the wrist. I'm sure they will keep us safe and sound during our trip.

Xiaolong: You're a quick learner. Let's go and buy some.

打午时水

> 小龙和大卫经过一个村子,看到很多人在水井旁打水,场面十分热闹,便走了过去,跟一位村民聊了起来。

大　卫:大叔,请问你们为什么排队打水?家里没有自来水吗?

村　民:当然有了。但这可不是普通的水。今天是端午节,大家排队是打午时水。

大　卫:午时水?

村　民:午时水是在端午节中午,从井里或河里打上来的水。每年端午节我们都要打午时水。

大　卫:小龙,午时是中午的意思吗?

小　龙:嗯,更确切地说,午时就是上午11点到下午1点这个时间段。中国古人计时是把一昼夜划分成十二个时段,叫十二时辰。一个时辰相当于现在的两个小

打午时水　Fetching Noonday Water　049

打午时水
Fetching Noonday Water

时，每个时辰用一个字命名。

大　卫：原来是这样。现在快12点了，怪不得大家都忙着打水呢。

村　民：中午12点是打午时水的正点。端午节我们会看准时间，在正点打水。

大　卫：那午时水有什么特别的吗？

村　民：有啊。一年中端午节这天阳气最盛，而午时又是一天中阳气最盛的时刻，所以午时水也叫"极阳水"。

大　卫：午时水用来干什么呢？

村　民：可干的事多啦。可以把午时水和白酒、雄黄混合，洒在屋里和房外四周来驱蚊虫，还可以给孩子们洗澡，防止他们生痱子或被蚊虫、毒蛇叮咬。用午时水洗脸还能明目。

大　卫：那这水能喝吗？

村　民：当然可以喝啦。做饭、煮汤、泡茶都可以。我们这儿有句古话，叫"午时水饮一嘴，胜过补药吃三年"。

大　卫：真有这么神奇吗？那我也来打一桶午时水，喝点儿试试。

村　民：好，你来试试吧。

Fetching Noonday Water

> While passing through a village, Xiaolong and David saw a lively crowd gathering around a well and fetching water. They went closer and started chatting with a villager.

David: Sir, I'm wondering why everybody is waiting in line to draw water? Don't you have running water at home?

Villager: Of course we do! But this isn't just ordinary water. Today is the Duanwu Festival and we're lining up to fetch noonday water.

David: Noonday water?

Villager: It's the water that we take from a well or a river at the hour of *wu* on the Duanwu Festival. We do this every year.

David: Xiaolong, does the hour of *wu* refer to midday?

Xiaolong: Yes. More precisely, it's the period between 11 a.m. and 1 p.m. Ancient Chinese people divided one day into twelve time periods called the twelve *shichen* (时辰). Each period was the equivalent of two hours of our time and named with a Chinese character.

David: Oh, I see. It's almost 12 o'clock now. No wonder everybody is busy fetching noonday water.

Villager: 12 o'clock at noon is actually the perfect time to fetch noonday water. During the Duanwu Festival, we all make sure to collect water at 12 o'clock sharp.

David: Is there anything special about noonday water?

Villager: Absolutely. The Duanwu Festival is the day of the year when the *yang qi*, also known as the *yang* energy, is the strongest, and the hour of *wu* is the time of the day when the yang *qi* reaches its apex. That's why noonday water is called "maximum *yang* water".

David: What else do you use this water for?

Villager: Plenty of ways to use it. For example, we mix noonday water with liquor and realgar, and spray it inside and around our houses in order to get rid of mosquitoes and other bugs. We also bath children with noonday water so that they don't get heat rash or get bitten by insects and snakes. It's good for eyesight as well, so we wash our faces with it.

David: Do you drink it?

Villager: Of course! We use it to cook, make soup, brew tea, anything. We have an old saying that goes, "One mouthful of noonday water is more useful than three years' worth of herbal tonics."

David: Wow. Is it really that amazing? I'd fetch some to drink, too.

Villager: Sure, give it a try.

贴午时符

> 喝完午时水,小龙和大卫继续在村子里溜达。大卫看到有一户人家门口贴了一张黄底红字的纸条。

大　卫: 小龙你看,这黄色的纸是什么?

小　龙: 这是贴纸符,也是端午的一种习俗。你还记得午时是什么时间吗?

大　卫: 是上午11点到下午1点。

小　龙: 没错。我再考考你,在午时打的水是午时水,那么午时贴在门上的符呢?

大　卫: 是午时符吗?

小　龙: 答对了。中国有些地方有端午节贴午时符的习俗。

大　卫: 贴午时符也是防灾驱病吧?

小　龙: 是的。你来看,这午时符上面写了一些字。人们午时把它们贴在家里不同的地方,用来辟邪。

贴午时符　Putting up Noonday Paper Charms

大　卫：这红色的字是用红色墨水写的吧。

小　龙：好像不是，应该是朱砂①吧。来，看看写了什么。

> 两人凑上前，念了起来。

大卫和小龙："五月五日午时书，破去官非口舌，蛇虫鼠蚁一切尽消除。"

大　卫：这些汉字是什么意思啊？

小　龙：我来给你讲一讲。先说第一句"五月五日午时书"。这里"书"是古汉语里的动词，是写的意思。我们今天还说书写呢。

大　卫：明白了。这句话的意思是说，这个符是在端午节午时写的。

小　龙：理解正确。"破去官非口舌"这句古汉语有点儿难理解，得好好解释一下。"破去"是"去除、化解"的意思。"官"在这里指"牢狱、官司"之类的事情；"非"的意思是"是非、纠纷"。"口舌"与言语有关。"官非口舌"是指因言语而引起的官司、牢狱之灾等不好的事情。"破去官非口舌"这句话意思就是，化解由于言语而引发的官

　　　　司、牢狱之灾。也就是说，写这个符，是希望生活
　　　　能够平安顺利，不要惹上麻烦。

大　卫：确实不太好懂。不过最后一部分我能看明白了，就
　　　　是消灭家里的老鼠、蚂蚁、蛇和害虫，对吗？

小　龙：没错。大卫，你再来看看这家大门上贴的是什么？

大　卫：哎哟，这家贴的是幅画像。这是谁呀？眼睛瞪得这
　　　　么大，看着很吓人。

小　龙：吓人就对了，这画的是钟馗。钟馗是道教[2]里的神
　　　　仙，能捉鬼驱邪。端午节贴钟馗像，也是希望辟邪
　　　　保平安。

大　卫：这么吓人的样子，鬼肯定也害怕。

小　龙：那当然了。我们再往前走走，看看还有什么有趣的
　　　　端午习俗。

大　卫：走，我们去看看。

注释：
① 朱砂：一种硫化物类矿物，主要成分为硫化汞（HgS）。朱砂呈鲜红色或暗红色，在中国也常被用作绘画颜料。
② 道教：发源于中国的本土宗教，对中国古代政治、经济和文化产生过深刻影响。

Putting up Noonday Paper Charms

> Xiaolong and David continued to stroll around the village after they had had a taste of noonday water. David noticed a piece of yellow paper with red writing pasted on the front door of a house.

David: Xiaolong, what's that yellow paper over there?

Xiaolong: Oh, these are paper charms. It's another Duanwu tradition. Do you remember what the hour of *wu* means?

David: It's the period from 11:00 a.m. to 1:00 p.m. at midday.

Xiaolong: Exactly. So, if water fetched at the hour of *wu* is called noonday water, what do you think paper charms that people paste on the front door at the hour of *wu* are called?

David: Noonday paper charms?

Xiaolong: Bingo! It's a tradition to paste noonday paper charms

贴午时符 Putting up Noonday Paper Charms

during the Duanwu Festival in some places.

David: It's also meant to prevent disasters and diseases, right?

Xiaolong: Correct. Look at this one. There're some characters written on the paper. People paste paper charms on the front door and other parts of the house at the hour of *wu* to drive away evils.

David: Were these red characters written in red ink?

Xiaolong: I don't think so. It must be cinnabar ink[1]. Let's see what it says.

The two went closer and read it aloud.

David, Xiaolong: *Wuyue wuri wushi shu, poqu guan fei koushe, she chong shu yi yiqie jin xiaochu* (五月五日午时书，破去官非口舌，蛇虫鼠蚁一切尽消除).

David: What does this mean?

Xiaolong: Let me explain it. The first part *wuyue wuri wushi shu* means "written at the hour of *wu* on the fifth day of the fifth lunar month". The last character *shu* is a verb in classical Chinese and it means "to write". You can also see it in the phrase *shuxie* (书写) that we use today, meaning "to write".

David: I get it. It says that this charm was written at the hour of *wu* during the Duanwu Festival.

Xiaolong: Exactly. *Poqu guan fei koushe,* is slightly more difficult to understand. I'll do my best to explain it. The characters *poqu* mean "to get rid of" or "to resolve". The character *guan* refers to things like "prison" or "lawsuit"; *fei* means "discord" or "dispute"; and the last two words *koushe* are related to accusation and argument. The phrase *guan fei koushe* means bad things like going to prison or being sued can happen to someone because of what they have said. So, this sentence means to sort out the problems caused by what a person has said. In other words, it expresses the wish for a peaceful life without any troubles.

David: This part is indeed hard to grasp. But I know what the last one means. It says to get rid of mice, ants, snakes, and pests in the house, right?

Xiaolong: You're quite right. Hey, David, look at the one on this door here.

David: Oh, it's a portrait. Who's that? His eyes are almost popping out, which gives me chills.

Xiaolong: He is supposed to be scary. This is a portrait of Zhong Kui, a Taoist[2] god who can capture ghosts and exorcise evils. People paste his portrait specifically to ward off evil spirits and protect their families.

David: He's so scary. I bet even ghosts are afraid of him.

Xiaolong: No doubt. Let's go and see what other interesting traditions we can find.

David: Sure.

Notes:

1. **Cinnabar**: A sulphide mineral consisting of mercury sulphide (HgS). It is bright red or dull red, and can be used as a painting pigment.

2. **Taoist**: Of or relating to Taoism, an indigenous religious tradition in China.

画额

> 小龙和大卫继续往前走,发现前面有一群孩子正围坐在一位四十多岁的妇女身旁。两人走上前去看热闹。

大　卫:小龙,你看!好多孩子围着那位阿姨。他们在干什么?

小　龙:看,她手里拿着毛笔,像是在孩子们的额头上写字。

大　卫:用毛笔在额头上写字?难道这也是端午节的习俗吗?

小　龙:这个我也是第一次看到,我们来问问吧。

大　卫:嗨,阿姨,您好!您在小朋友们额头上写什么呀?

阿　姨:哦,今天是端午节,我给他们画额呢。

小　龙:画额是在额头上画画吗?画什么呢?

阿　姨:就是用毛笔蘸上雄黄酒,在额头上写个"王"字。

大　卫:哇,这个"王"字很威风,也是辟邪的吧?

画额 Painting Children's Foreheads   063

画额 Painting Children's Foreheads

阿　姨：你这外国小伙子知道的还挺多呢。你说的没错，用雄黄酒画额就是为了赶走毒虫和邪气，保佑孩子们健康平安。

大　卫：为什么要写"王"字呢？

阿　姨：你看，这"王"字像不像老虎额头上的花纹？老虎很凶，在额头上写个"王"字，就是要借虎威镇住邪物。端午节给孩子们画额,是希望他们没病没灾,长命百岁啦。

大　卫:哦,原来是这个意思,让老虎把毒虫邪气吓走。

小　龙:借"百兽之王"的威猛,再加上雄黄酒,那更厉害了。

大　卫:我也想画一个。

小　龙:你没看到都是给小孩子画吗,哪有给大人画的?

阿　姨:其实大人也可以画。来,给你画一个。

大卫高高兴兴地让阿姨给自己画额。

小　龙:很好,特别威风。

阿　姨:小伙子,你们想不想学着给孩子们画额?

大　卫:太好了,我正想试试呢。

阿　姨:你看,很简单,蘸点儿雄黄酒,写个"王"字。

大卫高高兴兴接过阿姨手中的毛笔,继续给孩子们画额。

Painting Children's Foreheads

> As Xiaolong and David were walking around the village, David saw a group of children sitting around a lady in her forties. They went closer to see what was happening.

David: Xiaolong, look at those kids sitting around the lady. What are they doing?

Xiaolong: She's holding an ink brush. It seems to me she's writing something on the children's foreheads.

David: Writing on their foreheads? Is that also a Duanwu custom?

Xiaolong: I'm not sure. Actually, it's also my first time seeing this. Let's go and find out.

David: Hello, ma'am! What are you writing on their foreheads?

Lady: Oh, today's the Duanwu Festival, so I'm painting their foreheads.

Xiaolong: How is it done? Do you paint anything in particular?

Lady: Yes, we paint the character "王" (*wang*) which means king on their foreheads with realgar wine.

David: Wow, it looks impressive. It helps keep evils away, right?

Lady: Exactly. Young man, you know quite a lot. We paint their foreheads with realgar wine to drive away poisonous insects and evil spirits so that the children are safe and healthy.

David: But why do you write the character "王"?

Lady: Well, don't you think it looks like the stripes on a tiger's forehead? By painting the character "王" on kids' foreheads, we can borrow the power of fierce tigers to ward off evils. Doing this during the Duanwu Festival is to protect them from illnesses and disasters and ensure them a long life.

David: Oh, I see. You want to chase away pests and evil spirits by the power of a tiger.

Xiaolong: Exactly. With the power of "the king of all animals" and the efficacy of realgar wine, kids will get more protection.

David: I want to have a character "王" painted on my forehead, too!

Xiaolong: But they only paint it on children's foreheads, right? They don't paint for grown-ups.

Lady: It is no serious matter. Adults can get the paint as well. Take a seat. I'll paint it for you.

> Delighted, David sat down and let the lady paint on his forehead.

Xiaolong: Wow! You look very imposing now.

Lady: Young man, would you like to learn how to paint it for the children?

David: Yes, I'd like to. Thank you. That would be great. I was about to ask you.

Lady: It's simple. All you have to do is to dip the brush in realgar wine and then paint the character "王".

> David happily took the brush from the lady and continued to paint on the children's foreheads.

斗百草

> 小龙和大卫开心地画完额,不远处两个孩子玩的游戏又吸引了他们。

大　卫：小龙,你看,那两个孩子手里都拿着草。他们在玩什么游戏呀?

小　龙：在拉草玩,像是在比谁的力气大。

阿　姨：是的,这叫"斗百草",村里的小孩子都喜欢玩。

小　龙：这也是端午节游戏吗?我还真没玩过。有什么说法吗?

阿　姨：有哇。说起来,这跟采药有关。端午正好也是采草药的好时节。俗话说,"端午节前都是草,到了端午便成药"。

小　龙：那端午节采的草药是用来治什么特别的病吗?

阿　姨：端午节这天阳气最旺,草药的药性也最强,所以这

斗百草 Matching Herbs 069

斗百草 Matching Herbs

　　　　一天午时采的药，治很多病都很有效。
大　卫：那采草药和斗百草又是什么关系呢？
阿　姨：过去，端午采药的时候，大家会拿花草做游戏，
　　　　"斗百草"就是这么来的。他们这种玩法叫"武
　　　　斗"，就是两人各拔一根草，把草交叉，各自用双
　　　　手拉自己那根草的两头，使劲往后拽，谁能把对方

的草拉断，谁就赢了。

大　卫：这个好玩。小龙，我们也来"武斗"一下。我力气比你大，肯定能赢。

小　龙：我们斗斗看，还不知道谁会赢呢。

阿　姨：这个斗草可不光比力气，还要看谁选的草更韧，拉的时候也需要用巧劲。

大　卫：阿姨，我明白了。那等会儿我们来试试。

阿　姨：除了"武斗"，你们也可以试试"文斗"。

大　卫："文斗"是什么？

阿　姨："文斗"就是报花草名，谁报的多，谁就赢了。

大　卫："文斗"也很有意思，不过得知道很多花草名才行。

小　龙：那当然，比的就是学问。

大　卫：小龙，等我把中文练好，我们再"文斗"，现在我们还是"武斗"吧。

小　龙：好，我们现在就比试比试。

Matching Herbs

> Xiaolong and David finished painting the character " 王 " on kids' foreheads with great joy. Not far away, two children playing a game caught their attention.

David: Look, Xiaolong! Each of them is holding a plant in their hands. What kind of game is that?

Xiaolong: They are pulling at herbs. It seems that they are trying to see who is stronger.

Lady: Oh, that's called matching herbs. Kids in villages love to play this game.

Xiaolong: Is it a game specific to the Duanwu Festival? I've never played it.

Lady: Yes. People say it's related to the practice of picking medicinal herbs, and the Duanwu Festival is a great time for it. As the old saying goes, "Herbs are weeds before Duanwu; they become medicine after Duanwu."

Xiaolong: Why is that?

Lady: Herbs are most potent on the day of the Duanwu Festival since it's the time when *yang* energy reaches its fullest. The herbs picked on this day at the hour of *wu* are effective to cure many diseases.

David: But what does matching herbs have to do with harvesting medicinal herbs?

Lady: In the past, when people went picking herbs during the Duanwu Festival, they would play games with the grass and flowers for fun. That's how matching herbs came about. What you saw just now is called "strength matching". Two players each pluck a herb, putting one herb through the other, and then pull at the two ends of their own herb with strength. Whoever first breaks the stem of his opponent's herb is the winner.

David: It sounds fun. Xiaolong, shall we give it a try? I'm stronger than you, so I'll definitely win.

Xiaolong: Let's do it. Are you sure you'll win?

Lady: It's not all about strength. The technique is important, too. Besides, it also depends on whose herb is more durable.

David: I see. Thank you for the heads-up, ma'am. We'll go for a round.

Lady: Besides strength matching, you can also try words matching.

David: What does it mean?

Lady: It's a game of telling the names of plants, and the one who knows the most wins.

David: It sounds interesting, but it needs some knowledge about plants.

Xiaolong: Of course, it's a contest to see who knows more.

David: Let's do this after I learn more Chinese. For now, we can try the game of "strength matching".

Xiaolong: OK. Bring it on!

雄黄酒

> 第二天,小龙和大卫离开汨罗,来到端午之旅的第二站——湖北秭归。

小　龙:大卫,屈原的故乡秭归到了。这里山清水秀,是个好地方。

大　卫:这里真的很美呀。小龙,你看,也有人在划龙舟呢。

小　龙:是啊,这里除了划龙舟、吃粽子,还有其他有趣的端午习俗呢。

大　卫:那我们去看看。

小　龙:好,我们找个集市去逛逛,看看有什么新鲜事儿。大卫,你看,导航显示前面一千米左右的地方有个集市。

> 二人来到集市,看到有一个摊位正在卖一种黄色的酒。

雄黄酒　Realgar Wine　075

雄黄酒　Realgar Wine

小　龙：大卫，你猜这碗里装的是什么？

大　卫：黄黄的，有点酒味。好像和阿姨画额的东西一样，是雄黄酒吗？

小　龙：对，这就是雄黄酒。有些地方有端午节闻雄黄酒的习俗。

大　卫：嗯，我猜就像给孩子们画额一样，闻雄黄酒应该也是为了保平安。

小　龙：是的，这个雄黄酒是一种药酒。人们在端午闻它，也是为了辟邪、祛病、保平安。

大　卫：这个习俗有什么故事吗？

小　龙：有啊，这个习俗也和屈原有关，是关于屈原投江后的另一个故事。传说屈原投江后，江里有条蛟龙。

大　卫：所以老百姓往江里投粽子。

小　龙：另一个传说是，有个聪明的大夫往江里倒了一坛子雄黄酒，把蛟龙药晕了。后来，人们就相信雄黄酒可以祛恶辟邪，保佑平安。闻雄黄酒的习俗也就流传了下来。

大　卫：这种酒里是不是有麻醉药呀？

小　龙：应该没有。雄黄酒只是在白酒或黄酒里加入少量雄黄粉。雄黄是一种橘黄色的矿物质，含汞，有毒。但少量的雄黄能以毒攻毒、杀虫，还可以外用，治疗皮肤病。雄黄被中医用作解毒的一味中药呢。

大　卫：有这么多用处，那我得尝尝。

小　龙：只能闻闻，一般不喝，不过你可以尝尝是什么味道。

大　卫：啊，又苦又辣！

小　龙：雄黄酒有一定的毒性，所以一般都是用来涂擦或者洒在什么地方。端午节，长辈会在小孩子的额头、鼻子、耳朵等地方抹上雄黄酒，这样可以防蛇蝎蚊虫，辟邪防病。

大　卫：嗯，很有道理。这个气味应该可以驱赶蚊虫。

Realgar Wine

> The following day, Xiaolong and David left Miluo and headed to the second stop of their Duanwu journey—Zigui County in Hubei Province.

Xiaolong: David, we're now at Qu Yuan's hometown, Zigui County. It's a beautiful place, isn't it?

David: Yes, indeed. Look, Xiaolong! There's a dragon boat race going on.

Xiaolong: Oh, you're right. Besides the dragon boat racing and eating *zongzi*, there're other interesting Duanwu customs here.

David: Let's go and find out.

Xiaolong: Sure! Let's go to a market and see what's new here. The navigation app says there's a market about a kilometre away.

> The two of them arrived at the market where they noticed a stall selling a type of yellow liquor.

Xiaolong: David, guess what's in these bowls.

David: Hmm, it's yellowish and smells like alcohol. I think it's the same as what the lady used to paint kids' foreheads. Is it realgar wine?

Xiaolong: Exactly. Some people would like to sniff realgar wine during the Duanwu Festival as a traditional custom.

David: I guess it must be for protection, just like the character "王" painted on kids' foreheads.

Xiaolong: Sure. Realgar wine is a type of medicinal wine. People smell it to drive away evils, get rid of diseases, and stay safe.

David: Is there also a story behind this tradition?

Xiaolong: Of course. It's yet another custom related to Qu Yuan, more precisely, to his fall in the river. According to legend, after Qu Yuan drowned himself, a dragon came to the river.

David: Then the locals threw *zongzi* into the river to prevent it from feeding on his body. Am I right?

Xiaolong: Yes, it's the story of *zongzi*. Another legend says that a wise doctor poured a jug of realgar wine into the river, and drugged the dragon unconscious. Later, people believed that the liquor could ward off evils and keep them safe. The custom has been so passed down ever since.

David: Does realgar wine contain sedatives?

Xiaolong: I don't think so. It's just liquor or yellow rice wine dosed with a small amount of realgar powder. Realgar is a tangerine yellow, poisonous mineral that contains mercury. But a small amount of it can be used to kill insects or to cure skin diseases. It's a folk remedy of "fighting poison with poison". Because of that, it's used in traditional Chinese medicine as an antidote.

David: It's good for so many things, and I'd like to have a taste!

Xiaolong: Oh, usually people don't drink it. They only sniff it. But you can take a sip to see how it tastes.

David: Ugh, it's bitter and spicy!

Xiaolong: Since realgar wine has certain toxicity, people usually smear it on the skin or spray it somewhere. During the Duanwu Festival, elders rub it on children's foreheads, noses, and ears to protect them from snakes, scorpions, insects, as well as evils and illnesses.

David: That makes sense. The smell of realgar wine makes it an effective insect repellent.

避五毒

小　龙：大卫，你还记得我们看打午时水时，那个村民说把雄黄酒洒在屋内各个角落吗？那样做相当于杀菌消毒，能避五毒。

大　卫：五毒是什么？

小　龙：别急，听我慢慢给你讲。五毒是夏季比较常见的五种动物，古人认为它们有毒。我说说它们的样子，看你能不能猜出来？第一种，身体细长多节，每节上都长了一对脚，因为脚多，所以俗称"百脚"。

大　卫：我想应该是蜈蚣吧？

小　龙：答对了。第二种，长得像个青蛙，但四肢更短、更粗壮，表皮上疙疙瘩瘩的。

大　卫：应该是蟾蜍呀。

小　龙：看来还真难不倒你。你再猜猜第三种，"一根绳，草里藏，吃老鼠，人见慌"。

避五毒 Warding off Five Poisonous Creatures

大　卫：嗯……这个我猜不出来。

小　龙：蛇啊！

大　卫：哦，对呀，蛇吃老鼠。有些蛇确实是有毒的。还有另外两种呢？

小　龙：第四种，尾巴有个钩钩，见面蜇你一下，喜欢躲在暗处，最不爱晒太阳。

大　卫：应该是蝎子吧。

避五毒 Warding off Five Poisonous Creatures

小　龙：猜对了。而这第五种，就不用猜了，因为不同地区有不同说法，有的说是老虎，有的说是壁虎，还有的说是蜘蛛。

大　卫：难怪叫五毒，前面四种确实有毒。不过，第五种要是壁虎的话，就不对了。壁虎好像没毒吧，而且它还会捕食苍蝇、蚊子呢。

小　龙：这应该是古人对壁虎的误解，不完全科学。

大　卫：那为什么端午节的时候要避这五种动物呢？

小　龙：端午节前后，天气湿热，这五种动物经常出没。古人认为，它们不仅会伤人，还会传播疾病，所以才要避开它们。

大　卫：有道理。那怎么才能避开它们呢？

小　龙：清洁卫生、洒雄黄酒都是很好的办法。

大　卫：我闻了雄黄酒，也可以避五毒了吧。

小　龙：希望如此。刚才我们说到的五毒，大多有毒性而且外表吓人，人们就利用它们的形象来驱赶害虫、避开邪气，免受毒虫侵扰，保护身体健康。民间习俗中有两种有趣的方法避五毒，象征性地消灭它们，比如贴五毒图和吃五毒饼。

大　卫：具体怎么做呢？

小　龙：贴五毒图就是把五毒画在纸上，贴在家里，再用针刺在五毒上面。这样一来，五毒就被刺死，不会出来害人了。五毒饼是表面装饰有五毒图案的糕点，把这些糕点吃下去，也就把五毒消灭啦。

大　卫：这个习俗好有趣。

小　龙：在民间这种精神胜利法很多，叫以毒攻毒。比如，给小孩子穿五毒衣，就是在衣服上绣上五毒图案，吓走五毒，不让疾病靠近小孩。还有佩戴五毒钱币，在门窗上张贴五毒剪纸，都是以毒攻毒的办法。

大　卫：看来避五毒的办法还真不少。要不，我们也去吃点儿五毒饼避避毒吧。

小　龙：好啊，我们去找找，看有没有卖五毒饼的。

Warding off Five Poisonous Creatures

Xiaolong: David, do you remember when we saw people fetching noonday water, the villager told us they sprayed realgar wine around the house? By doing so, they can disinfect their surroundings and ward off *wudu* (五毒), meaning five poisonous creatures.

David: What're the five poisonous creatures?

Xiaolong: Wait a minute. I'll tell you all about it. They're often found during summer and were thought to be poisonous. I'll describe them, and you can guess what they are. The first one has a long and thin body formed of many segments with a pair of legs on each segment. Because it has so many legs, it's also called "hundred legs".

David: Centipede, I guess. Am I right?

Xiaolong: Bingo! Now, the second one. It resembles a frog but has shorter, stouter limbs and bumpy skin.

David: Isn't it the toad?

Xiaolong: Correct. It seems too easy for you. Let's take it up a notch with a riddle, and see if you can guess the third animal. "It's like a rope, hidden in grass, and it feeds on rats, and frightens us."

David: Hmm... I don't know this one.

Xiaolong: It's the snake!

David: Oh, you're right! Snakes do eat rats. Some of them are indeed venomous. What about the other two creatures?

Xiaolong: The fourth one has a tail with a small hook. When you cross paths, it will sting you. It likes hiding in dark places and hates sunlight.

David: I think it's the scorpion.

Xiaolong: Exactly. As for the last one, I will spare you the guessing because people from different regions have different opinions about what it is. Some say it's the tiger, others say it's the spider or the gecko.

David: No wonder they are called five poisonous creatures. The first four are indeed venomous. But if the fifth one is the gecko, it would be wrong to call them five poisonous creatures. I believe geckos are harmless. On top of that, they prey on flies and mosquitoes.

Xiaolong: I would say that ancient Chinese people had some misconceptions about geckos and wrongly took them as being poisonous.

David: Why do people ward off the five poisonous creatures during the Duanwu Festival?

Xiaolong: Around the Duanwu Festival, the weather is hot and humid, so those five creatures will start creeping around. It was believed that they would hurt people and transmit diseases. That's why ancient people believed that they should keep the five creatures at a distance.

David: Fair enough. But how do you do that?

Xiaolong: Cleaning up and spraying realgar wine are all good solutions.

David: Since I've already sniffed realgar wine, I suppose they'll stay away from me.

Xiaolong: Hopefully, they will. We've already mentioned that the five poisonous creatures are mostly venomous and scary looking. It's precisely for this reason that people use their images to keep away pests and evil spirits. In doing so, people will stay safe and well. According to folk customs, there are two inventive methods for driving away the spirit of the five poisonous creatures. You can do this by putting up their pictures or eating cakes with the images of the five creatures.

David: Could you be more specific?

Xiaolong: Sure. People first draw the five poisonous creatures on a piece of paper and then paste it on the wall. After that, prick the drawings with needles to symbolise killing the creatures so they won't do any harm. Well, eating cakes with their images on is another symbolic way to get rid of the poisonous creatures.

David: It sounds interesting.

Xiaolong: It's a spiritual victory, also known as combating poison with poison. There're many examples in folk culture. One of them is to dress children in clothes with *wudu* patterns to scare off poisonous creatures and protect children from getting sick. Others include wearing coins engraved with *wudu* images and pasting paper cuts with *wudu* patterns on doors and windows.

David: There seems to be quite a few ways to ward off the poisonous creatures. Why don't we have some cakes to scare them away, too?

Xiaolong: Good idea. Let's get going to find some.

食五黄

> 小龙和大卫没有找到五毒饼。他们来到一家餐馆,门口的招牌上写着:"五月五,五黄三白过端午。"

大　卫:小龙,你看,这上面写着"五黄三白过端午","五黄三白"是什么?

小　龙:这是端午节常吃的时令食物。"五黄"是五种名字里带"黄"字的食物。

大　卫:那"三白"就是三种名字里带"白"字的食物了吧?是哪些食物呢?

小　龙:不急,我们先点个"五黄"套餐吧,看看会上些什么菜。我们再聊聊"三白",怎么样?

大　卫:好呀,看看我们能吃上什么"五黄"。

> 两人点了"五黄"套餐。不一会儿,服务员端上来四道菜、一小坛酒。

大　卫：这应该是雄黄酒吧？雄黄酒名字里就有个"黄"字。

小　龙：不是的，雄黄酒有毒性，不会在饭店里卖的。这是黄酒，也带个"黄"字。

大　卫：闻着挺香的，我来尝一口。这个酒好，有点儿甜，是米做的吧？

小　龙：是的，一般用糯米做黄酒。这种酒适量饮用有益健康。你知道吗？黄酒是中国特有的酒，有4000年的历史了。听说它和啤酒、葡萄酒并称世界上最古老的三大酒呢。

食五黄 Eating Five Healthy Foods

大　卫：是吗？那我可要再喝一些。

小　龙：你再看看这几道菜。

大　卫：这是黄瓜，有"黄"字。这切开的是煮鸡蛋吧？嗯，蛋黄是黄的。不过这黄颜色怎么这么深呀？

小　龙：这不是鸡蛋，是咸鸭蛋。腌过的蛋黄是深黄色的。

大　卫：那这两道菜是鱼呀，它们也不太黄呀。

小　龙：这是黄鱼和黄鳝，黄鱼是海鱼，黄鳝是淡水鱼。

大　卫：哦，它们的名字里面都有个"黄"字。

小　龙：是的，"五黄"就是黄酒、黄瓜、咸鸭蛋黄、黄鱼和黄鳝。

大　卫：那"三白"是什么呢？

小　龙："三白"指茭白、白切肉和咸蛋白（或白豆腐），也是端午节吃的。不过各地的"三白"不太一样。吃"五黄"是最普遍的习俗。

大　卫：为什么要在端午节的时候吃"五黄三白"呢？

小　龙：古人认为，一年中阳气最旺盛的日子就在端午时节，加上天气闷热，人比较容易烦躁上火，需要通过饮食调理，达到养生的目的。

大　卫：吃这些食物能去火、养生吗？

小　龙：应该可以吧。这些时令食物，营养丰富，大多清热解毒，有利于健康。比如，端午期间的黄鳝最肥美，营养丰富，所以南方民间有"端午黄鳝赛人参"的说法。

大　卫：看来"五黄三白过端午"很有道理。下次我要尝尝"三白"。

小　龙：好，吃了"五黄"，我们也算过了端午节啦。干杯！

Eating Five Healthy Foods

Xiaolong and David couldn't find *wudu* cakes. They arrived at a restaurant and noticed a sign at the entrance that says "Come in to have some *wuhuang* and *sanbai* to celebrate the Duanwu Festival on May the 5th".

David: Xiaolong, take a look at the sign. What do they mean by *wuhuang* (五黄) and *sanbai* (三白)?

Xiaolong: They refer to the seasonal healthy foods people eat during the Duanwu Festival. *Wuhuang* stands for five kinds of foods with the Chinese character *huang* (黄) in their names. *Huang* means yellow.

David: Then I assume *sanbai* refers to three types of foods with the character *bai* (白) or white, in their names. Can you tell me what foods are included?

Xiaolong: There's no rush, David. Let's first order the *wuhuang* meal to see what dishes they bring us. After that, we can talk about *sanbai*. What do you say?

David: Okay. I'm wondering what five foods we'll get.

> Xiaolong ordered the *wuhuang* meal. Soon, a waiter served them four dishes and a jug of wine.

David: This must be realgar wine, and there's a *huang* in its name.

Xiaolong: You've got it wrong this time. You know, realgar wine is somewhat toxic, restaurants can't serve it. This is actually yellow wine, or *huangjiu* in Chinese. Its name contains the character *huang* as well.

David: Ah, but it smells good. Let me try some. Aha, it tastes great, slightly sweet. It's made from rice, isn't it?

Xiaolong: Yes. It's usually brewed from glutinous rice, which makes it healthy. Yellow wine is specific to China and it has a history of 4,000 years. It's said that it's one of the oldest alcoholic drinks in the world together with beer and wine.

David: Really? In that case, I'd like some more.

Xiaolong: Now let's see if you can recognize the dishes.

David: Well, this is cucumber. I know it's called *huanggua* (黄瓜) in Chinese. These over here must be sliced boiled eggs. Er, yolk is called *danhuang* (蛋黄). But how come the yolk looks different?

Xiaolong: They aren't chicken eggs but salted duck eggs. The yolk turned dark yellow because the eggs have been soaked in brine.

David: What about the other two dishes of fish? They don't look so yellow to me.

Xiaolong: This one is *huangyu* (黄鱼), a type of sea fish. And the other is *huangshan* (黄鳝), ricefield eel, a yellowish freshwater fish.

David: I see. They all have the character *huang* in their names.

Xiaolong: Right.

David: Then what is *sanbai*?

Xiaolong: *Sanbai*, three healthy foods with the Chinese character bai (白) or white in their names, usually refers to water bamboo shoots, boiled pork slices, and egg whites of salted duck eggs or tofu. *Sanbai* food varies from place to place. The custom of eating *wuhuang* is the most common for the Duanwu Festival.

David: And why do people eat *wuhuang* and *sanbai* during the Duanwu Festival?

Xiaolong: In ancient times, people believed that Duanwu was the day of the year when *yang* energy reached its peak. This, combined with the sultry weather, put people at risk of suffering from excessive internal heat. It became necessary to adjust one's diet to avoid the internal heat and stay healthy.

David: So, eating *wuhuang* and *sanbai* can reduce internal heat and keep one healthy?

Xiaolong: It's believed so. These seasonal foods aren't only nutritious but can clear heat and eliminate toxins. Take eels as an example. It's best to catch them around the Duanwu Festival when they are most tender and nutrient-rich. People in southern China say that "ricefield eels caught during Duanwu are more nutritious than ginseng".

David: So, there are many reasons why people eat *wuhuang* and *sanbai* during the Duanwu Festival. Next time I'll try *sanbai*.

Xiaolong: Sure. Now let's eat *wuhuang* to celebrate the Duanwu Festival. Cheers!

西塞神舟会

> 端午假期第三天,小龙和大卫来到了端午之旅的第三站——黄石。

小　龙:大卫,我们去看有名的西塞神舟会吧。

大　卫:小龙,神舟就是龙舟吗?

小　龙:这里的神舟是用竹子扎的龙舟,很有气势。不过这个龙舟不是让人划的,而是要恭恭敬敬送到长江里,让它顺江漂向大海。

大　卫:这是为什么?

小　龙:等下你就明白了。我们要去的是西塞山区的道士洑村,那里每年从农历四月初八到五月十八,都会举办隆重的西塞神舟会,会有制作神舟、唱大戏、巡游、送神舟下水等很多活动。

大　卫:那不是要40天吗?

小　龙：是的，这里的端午活动是全国持续时间最长的。

大　卫：小龙，你看，神舟旁边的桌子上有很多神仙像呢。

小　龙：哦，那种桌子叫香案，上面供奉神仙像。

大　卫：很多人正在磕头礼拜呢。

小　龙：是的，这里原先供奉了屈原，叫屈原宫，后来放了神舟，就叫神舟宫。可惜我们没赶上端午节的神舟启动仪式，不过能看到大家来向神舟许愿求福也挺不错的。

> 小龙和大卫来到了道士洑村。正值端午节，游客很多，村子里很热闹。二人前往西塞山下神舟宫，看到了那艘龙形神舟。

大　卫：你看，这神舟真漂亮，船上还有楼台呢，这个和那种划的龙舟一点儿都不一样。龙的嘴巴、耳朵，还有尾巴，真夸张呀。

小　龙：这神舟是用竹篾编的，编好之后再在上面糊上彩纸等装饰。这个神舟很大，再加上这些神仙像的分量，出宫的时候得16名年轻小伙子一起抬。

大　卫：那很壮观呀。这个得有六七米长吧。

小　龙：大约长7米，宽2米，高5米。我们去找个神舟会的人问问吧。

> 小龙找来一位在神舟会工作的大叔。

小　龙：大叔，我们是来看西塞神舟会的。

大　叔：你们来早了，现在还不热闹，要到五月十五以后才热闹呢。

大　卫：啊，来早了？现在不是端午节吗？

大　叔：是这样的，我们这里自古有五月初五过"小端午"，十五过"大端午"的说法。不过现在大多数地方已经不过"大端午"了。我们西塞神舟会活动实际上是跨着"小端午"和"大端午"两个节。

小　龙：我可是第一次听说要过两个端午。

大　卫：大叔，这些神仙像都是谁呀？

大　叔：它们是天上、人间、冥界的各路神仙，一共有108位。最重要的舟神叫黑爷，他率领其他107位神仙，收了百毒，然后押解它们入江出海，保佑百姓平安。

大　卫：这么多神仙像，要扎很长时间吧？

大　叔：是的，我们从农历四月初八开始扎制神舟和神仙像，要做到五月初四，将近一个月才能完成呢。

小　龙：神舟和神仙像都做得很精致。

西塞神舟 The Xisai Sacred Boat

大　叔：都是上一辈师傅手把手教我们的，不过现在用的材料和以前已经大不一样了。听我爷爷说，以前，神冠都是用纯银打造的，衣服是用棉布做的。我们现在是用竹篾扎，用纸糊。

大　卫：这样好，更节约环保。我有个问题，为什么是108位神仙像呢？

大　叔：听老人说，是因为一年有十二个月，二十四节气①，七十二候②。这些数字加在一起正好等于108，所以我们就扎108位神仙像。这些都是祖祖辈辈传下来的。这神舟的造型自古没变,楼台亭榭按照原样精心扎制。我们还保留着100多年前的扎制图纸呢。

大　卫：那就是说我们现在看到的神舟和100多年前的一样了。太厉害了。这些神仙像都要放到神舟上吗？

大　叔：是的。等到五月十五,我们要将扎好的108位神仙像请上神舟,分别放在舟首、中仓和尾仓里。每个神仙都有自己的位置,不能随便乱放。五月十六神舟会出宫巡游。

小　龙：神舟还要出宫巡游？

大　叔：是呀。这是神舟会最隆重的部分。家家户户都要在门边悬挂菖蒲、艾叶,门口设香案,摆供品。神舟巡游经过时,家家都要放鞭炮迎接,撒茶米祭拜。

小　龙：神舟为什么要出宫巡游？

大　叔：神舟出游的目的,一是送福,二是收毒,三是娱神。

大　卫：唉,可惜我们明天就得回去,这么热闹的场面看不到了。

大　叔：没关系,想看热闹的话,可以明年五月十五来。最热闹的是五月十八神舟"登江"。那天江边大堤上人山人海，十里八村的人都来观看。

小　龙：“登江”是什么？

大　叔：是大家恭恭敬敬送神舟和108位神仙入江。前有人开路，后有人护送，中间是16名年轻小伙子抬着神舟送入长江，由水流带着神舟沿江而下，东流入海。

小　龙：象征着把百毒送走，是吗？

大　叔：是的，百毒就在108位神仙的押解下，远离我们道士洑，驶向大海。

大　卫：大叔，我们明年一定来看神舟登江。

小　龙：谢谢大叔给我们讲解西塞神舟会。明年五月十五我们一定来。

注释：

① 二十四节气：中国传统历法中特定的二十四个节令，每月两个节气。二十四节气反映了中国的自然节律变化，指导农耕生产，也是内容丰富的民俗文化系统。2016年，二十四节气被列入联合国教科文组织的《人类非物质文化遗产代表作名录》。

② 七十二候：中国传统历法的重要补充，主要用来说明节气变化，指导农事活动。

The Xisai Sacred Boat Ceremony

> On the third day of the Duanwu holiday, Xiaolong and David arrived at the third stop on their Duanwu journey — Huangshi.

Xiaolong: David, let's go to see the famous Xisai Sacred Boat Ceremony.

David: Xiaolong, is the Sacred Boat a dragon boat, too?

Xiaolong: Not exactly the same as what we've seen before. The one they have here is made of bamboo and looks quite beautiful and majestic. It's not for rowing. Instead, people send it off on the Yangtze River so that it can float away to the sea.

David: Why do they do that?

Xiaolong: You'll see when we get there. We're going to Daoshifu, a village in Xisaishanqu. Every year from the eighth day of the fourth lunar month to the eighteenth of the fifth month, the locals hold the grand Xisai Sacred Boat Ceremony. There're plenty of activities, like making the Sacred Boat, singing the traditional opera, holding parades, and launching the Sacred Boat on water.

David: So, the ceremony actually lasts 40 days?

Xiaolong: Yes. They have the longest celebration of the Duanwu Festival.

Xiaolong and David arrived at Daoshifu. The village was buzzing with life and bustling with visitors during the Duanwu Festival. They headed towards the Sacred Boat Palace at the foot of Xisai Mountain where they finally saw the dragon-shaped Sacred Boat.

David: Look, Xiaolong. There're many statues of gods on the table next to the Sacred Boat.

Xiaolong: Well, that table is called the incense altar, on which statues of gods are enshrined. Beside the altar are paper figurines of different gods.

David: Many people are kowtowing and praying in front of the altar.

Xiaolong: Right. This place was originally called Qu Yuan Palace where Qu Yuan used to be worshipped. Later, the Sacred Boat was placed here, so it was renamed the Sacred Boat Palace. It's a pity we missed the opening ceremony they held during the Duanwu Festival. Still, it's good to see people coming for the blessing of the Sacred Boat.

David: Yes, indeed. Look at this dragon boat, Xiaolong. It's so beautiful! There's even a tower on it. Now I understand why you said it was different from those for rowing. The dragon's mouth, ears, and tail are so impressive!

Xiaolong: The body of the boat is woven from bamboo strips. And then people would paste coloured paper and other ornaments on the surface. This boat is so large that sixteen sturdy young men are needed to carry it out of the palace.

David: That's quite a scene. The boat must be six or seven metres long.

Xiaolong: Specifically, it's almost seven metres long, two metres wide, and five metres tall. Let's look for a local to tell us more about it.

> Xiaolong found a staff member who worked for the Sacred Boat Ceremony.

Xiaolong: Hi. We're here to see the Xisai Sacred Boat Ceremony.

Staff Member: Oh, you're early. The most fun part hasn't started yet. Only after the fifteenth of the fifth lunar month do things liven up.

David: Early? But isn't it the Duanwu Festival already?

Staff Member: Here's the thing. The local tradition has always been to celebrate the "first Duanwu Festival" on the fifth of the fifth lunar month and then the "second Duanwu Festival" on the fifteenth. But the latter isn't celebrated in other places any more. The Xisai Sacred Boat Ceremony actually spans both festivals.

Xiaolong: I see. This is the first time I hear about two Duanwu festivals.

David: Sir, who do those figurines represent?

Staff Member: They are 108 gods in the heaven, the human world, and the underworld. The most important among them is called Lord Hei. He leads the other 107 gods to gather all the poisons and cast them out in the river to be carried away to the sea. They do so to keep people safe.

David: Making so many paper figurines must take a great deal of time.

Staff Member: It surely does. We begin making the Sacred Boat and figurines of gods on the eighth of the fourth lunar month and do this until the fourth of the fifth lunar month. We need almost one month to get everything done.

Xiaolong: The boat and the figurines of gods are all so exquisitely made.

Staff Member: We inherited the craftsmanship from our elders. But the materials we use now are very different from those of the past. My grandfather told me that pure silver was used for the crowns of the gods and cotton cloth for their costumes. Now we use bamboo strips and paper.

David: That's better, because it's more cost-effective and environmentally friendly, isn't it? Well, I have a question. Why are there 108 gods?

Staff Member: It's because there are twelve months, twenty-four solar terms[1], and seventy-two seasonal indicators[2] for one year. Those numbers all add up to 108, so we make 108 gods. This has all been passed down from generation to generation. The design of the Sacred Boat hasn't changed since ancient times, and the tower on it is still carefully made according to the original model. We've also preserved the design paper used over 100 years ago.

David: That means the boat we see now is the same as it was more than 100 years ago. This is amazing! Do you have to fit all those gods on the boat?

Staff Member: Yes. On the fifteenth of the fifth lunar month, we piously fit the gods on the boat, placing them at the front, middle, and back respectively. Each god has his own position, so we can't put them at random. On the sixteenth day, the Sacred Boat will come out of the palace for the parade.

Xiaolong: You take the Sacred Boat on a parade?

Staff Member: That's right. It's the most solemn part of the ceremony. Every household has to hang sweet flags and mugwort on the front door and set up an incense altar with offerings at the door. When the boat stops by a house, people set off firecrackers to welcome it, and throw tea and rice to pay reverence.

Xiaolong: And why does the boat leave the palace for the parade?

Staff Member: For three reasons: to give blessings, to get rid of poisons, and to entertain the gods.

David: It's a pity that we have to leave tomorrow, and we will miss such an exciting sight.

Staff Member: All right then. If you want to catch the most entertaining part, you may come back next year on the fifteenth of the fifth lunar month. The most thrilling part is on the eighteenth when the boat gets off to a down-the-rive start. The river embankment is packed with people from the surrounding villages to watch the event.

Xiaolong: What do you mean by the "down-the-river start"?

Staff Member: It means sending the Sacred Boat and the 108 gods off to the river. There will be people in front of the boat to lead the way and people behind the boat to escort it and the gods. Sixteen sturdy young men will carry the boat to the Yangtze River to let the water carry it down and all the way eastward towards the sea.

Xiaolong: Does it symbolise warding off the poisons?

Staff Member: Exactly. Under the watch of the 108 gods, those poisons leave Daoshifu Village and head out to the sea.

David: Sir, next year we'll be here when the Sacred Boat starts floating down the river.

Xiaolong: Thank you for telling us about the Xisai Sacred Boat

Ceremony. We'll certainly come again next year.

Notes:

1. Twenty-four solar terms: According to the traditional Chinese calendar, the twenty-four solar terms are twenty-four periods that make up one year. Each month contains two such terms. The twenty-four solar terms reflect the changes in climate and natural phenomena throughout a year in China, functioning as important guidance on agriculture production. They are also a rich cultural system of folklore and were inscribed on UNESCO's Representative List of the Intangible Cultural Heritage of Humanity in 2016.

2. Seventy-two seasonal indicators: As an important addition to the traditional Chinese calendar, the seventy-two seasonal indicators can be used to explain the changes during each season and guide agricultural activities.

沐兰汤

> 傍晚，小龙和大卫看完西塞神舟会，回到酒店。

小　龙：大卫，今天走了一天，累了吧？想不想去解解乏呢？

大　卫：解乏？是什么意思？

小　龙：就是解除困乏、消除疲劳的意思。

大　卫：好啊，去什么地方？

小　龙：去沐兰汤吧。"沐"是沐浴，也就是我们常说的泡澡，"兰汤"是兰草水，"沐兰汤"就是拿兰草水洗澡的意思，这也是端午节的一个活动。

大　卫：太好了，我们去体验一下。

> 小龙和大卫来到酒店的水疗馆洗了兰汤浴。

小　龙：大卫，感觉怎么样？

沐兰汤　Having Herbal Baths

大　卫：真的很舒服。浴池里的水有种特殊的香气，不知道是什么？

小　龙：是兰草的香味。说到"兰汤"中的"兰"字，有人误认为是兰花，实际是兰草，也就是佩兰或者泽兰，都是中医用的草药。

大　卫：哦，是中草药啊。那拿草药水洗澡是不是也能驱病呢？

小　龙：是的。端午节是古人的卫生防疫节。古人用洗澡的方式来清洁身体、驱邪防病。在古代，端午节也被称为"浴兰节"。

大　卫：挺有道理的，洗完澡确实很舒服。

小　龙：古代端午有采草药的习俗。采来的草药可以用来治病，兰草之类还可以用来煮水洗澡。据说，正午用兰汤洗澡，效果最好。

大　卫：明白了。正午气温最高，阳气最盛，这时候沐兰汤，驱邪防病的效果自然是最好的。

小　龙：你学得还挺快。

大　卫：可惜现在是晚上了，不过，效果也不错。那我们下一站去哪里？

小　龙：回苏州，继续体验端午文化习俗。苏州的端午习俗也不少呢。

大　卫：好，那我们明天就回去，完成四地游最后一站的端午体验。

Having Herbal Baths

In the evening, Xiaolong and David returned to the hotel after seeing the Xisai Sacred Boat Ceremony.

Xiaolong: David, we walked around all day. I bet you're tired, too. It's time to *jiefa* (解乏).

David: *Jiefa*? What does that mean in Chinese?

Xiaolong: It means to relieve fatigue and refresh ourselves.

David: Sounds good to me. Where are we going?

Xiaolong: Let's try *mu lantang* (沐兰汤). *Mu* means "to bath". It's also known as *paozao*, the Chinese phrase for "to soak in a tub". And *lantang* is herbal water. *Mu lantang* means to take a bath in herbal water, which is a traditional activity during the Duanwu Festival as well.

David: That's fantastic! Let's go!

> Xiaolong and David had a herbal bath at the hotel's spa.

Xiaolong: So, David, what do you think of it?

David: It feels great. And the water in the tub has a particular aroma. What's it?

Xiaolong: That's the smell of eupatorium. Oh, that reminds me. Many people think that the character *lan* in *lantang* refers to the phrase *lanhua* (兰花), which means orchid. But it actually comes from *lancao* (兰草), the Chinese for eupatorium. To be more specific, it includes two species of plants: the eupatorium fortunei herb and the hirsute shiny bugleweed herb. Both of them are used in traditional Chinese medicine.

David: I see. It's a medicinal herb. Then, does bathing in herbal water help in treating diseases?

Xiaolong: Definitely. You see, the Duanwu Festival was indeed intended for health in ancient times. Our ancestors took baths to cleanse their bodies, to ward off evils, and to prevent diseases. In fact, another name for the

Duanwu Festival was the "Herbal Bath Festival".

David: That's true. I do feel refreshed after the bath.

Xiaolong: People used to pick medicinal herbs during the Duanwu Festival. Besides using those herbs to treat diseases, they also added plants like eupatorium to the bathwater. It was said that bathing at noon rendered the best efficacy.

David: Understood. Noon is the hottest part of the day when *yang* energy reaches its peak. So, noon is the perfect time for a herbal bath and warding off evils.

Xiaolong: Right. You're a fast learner.

David: It's already night time now. But, anyway, the bath was nice. What's our next destination?

Xiaolong: We're returning to Suzhou. We'll continue to appreciate the culture of the Duanwu Festival there. Suzhou has quite a few Duanwu customs we can explore.

David: Okay. We'll leave tomorrow and head to the fourth and last stop on our Duanwu trip.

放纸鸢

> 小龙和大卫回到苏州,约好第二天下午去体验当地的端午习俗。第二天下午,他们来到一个公园,看到有人在放风筝。

大　卫:小龙,你看,公园里有人在放风筝呢。

小　龙:看到了。放风筝也是一个端午习俗。

大　卫:放风筝不是很常见吗?春天、秋天很多人都在公园放风筝呀。这也跟端午节有关吗?

小　龙:是的。许多地方都有端午放风筝的习俗。放风筝以前叫"放纸鸢"。

大　卫:风筝为什么要叫纸鸢呢?

小　龙:这得说到风筝的起源。鸢是一种像老鹰的鸟。2000多年前,有人用木头模仿鸢的形状做成木鸢,用作战争时期的通信工具。后来,进一步发展,木鸢带上火药,就成了进攻的武器。后来做木鸢的材料变

放纸鸢 Flying Kites

了，竹子取代了木头，把纸糊在上面，就叫纸鸢。它们的用途也变了，从战争工具变成春天里孩子们的玩具。

大　卫：纸鸢是什么时候变成玩具的呢？

小　龙：在距今1300多年的唐朝，放纸鸢就变成娱乐活动了。后来，有人在纸鸢上加上哨子，在空中飞起来发出的声音像是古筝的声音，所以就改名叫风筝。

大　卫：为什么在端午节放风筝呢？

小　龙：也是为了辟邪免灾。放风筝还有个别名叫"放殃"。"殃"是指祸害，"放殃"就是送走祸害的意思。在端午节放风筝，就是为了让不好的事情随风而去。

大　卫：原来放风筝还有这层意思，真有趣。

小　龙：是的。还有些人认为放风筝会带来好运，风筝放得越高，运气越好。

大　卫：那我们也去放吧！小龙，那边有卖风筝的。我们去买一个。

> 两人来到一处卖风筝的摊位。

小　龙：大卫，你瞧，这么多漂亮的风筝。

大　卫：有老鹰、蝴蝶、金鱼、蜻蜓，造型真多。好精致呀！这些风筝是怎么做出来的？

小　龙：风筝制作是中国的传统手工艺。简单说，先用竹篾扎成各种形状的骨架，然后在骨架上糊上纸或绢，再用长线系紧。扎风筝需要技巧，平衡是关键。

大　卫：小龙，你快看。那边有人把风筝撕破了。

小　龙：那是故意的，这也是一种民俗。

大　卫：他们为什么要这样做呢？

小　龙：很早以前，人们放完风筝收回来以后，都要将纸撕掉，只留下一个空的骨架带回家。等到明年端午，再拿出来糊上纸，重新放飞。你想，如果将风筝完好无损地带回家，那不就等于又把灾祸带回家了么？

大　卫：嗯，有道理。放完风筝还要把糊在上面的纸撕掉才行，否则不吉利。走，我们去放风筝吧。看看我们的风筝能不能越飞越高，为我们带来好运。

小　龙：我相信我们的风筝一定会飞得很高的！

Flying Kites

Xiaolong and David returned to Suzhou to explore the local Duanwu customs. The next afternoon, they entered a park and saw people flying kites.

David: Xiaolong, look at all these people flying kites!

Xiaolong: Yes. Flying kites is another traditional custom for the Duanwu Festival.

David: Isn't kite flying very common? A lot of people do that in parks during spring and autumn. How is it related to the Duanwu Festival?

Xiaolong: Let me explain it to you then. People fly kites during the Duanwu Festival in many places. Kites were called *zhiyuan* (纸鸢) in the past.

David: Why were they called *zhiyuan*?

Xiaolong: Well, we need to talk about the origins of the kite first. *Yuan* in Chinese is a type of bird that looks like an eagle. More than two thousand years ago, people carved wood into the shape of the bird and used it to carry messages during wartime. Then people started tying gunpowder packets to this wooden tool, converting it into a weapon. Later, the materials for making kites changed, and so did its purpose. Bamboo replaced wood, and the bamboo frame was pasted with paper, or *zhi* in Chinese. People called the new invention *zhiyuan*, and it became a toy for children in spring rather than a tool of war.

David: When did it become a toy?

Xiaolong: Flying *zhiyuan* became a fun activity in the Tang Dynasty over 1,300 years ago. Later, people attached whistles to the toy. The sound they made while flying up in the sky resembled that of *guzheng* (古筝), a stringed instrument. So, a new name for *zhiyuan* was coined by combining the characters *feng* (风 wind) and *zheng*, as in *guzheng*.

David: But why do people fly kites during the Duanwu Festival?

Xiaolong: Once again, the purpose is to drive away evils and prevent disasters. In fact, there is another name for flying kites, that is, *fangyang* (放殃). *Yang* means "disaster", and *fang* means "to release" in this context, so *fangyang* implies "to send off disasters". People fly kites during the Duanwu Festival to let bad things be taken away by the wind.

David: I didn't know there was such a deep meaning behind the practice of flying kites. It's really interesting.

Xiaolong: Yes, it is. Some people even believe that flying kites will bring good luck to them; the higher their kites go, the more luck they'll get.

David: Really? Then let's waste no more time and fly a kite, too! Look, Xiaolong. They are selling kites over there. Let's go to have a look!

> They came to a stall that sold kites.

Xiaolong: Look at all these beautiful kites!

David: They come in so many shapes: eagles, butterflies,

goldfish, and dragonflies. How exquisite! How are they made?

Xiaolong: Kite making is a traditional Chinese handicraft. There're basically three steps. First, bend thin bamboo strips into frames of different shapes, then paste paper or silk on the frame, and finally, attach a long string to it. Making kites isn't so easy. It requires skills, and a key point is to balance the kite.

David: Look, Xiaolong. Why are those people tearing up their kites?

Xiaolong: They do it on purpose. That's a folk custom, too.

David: Why would they do that?

Xiaolong: When people finished flying kites in old days, they would rip off the paper and only bring the bare frame back home. During the next Duanwu Festival, they would paste new paper on the frame and take the kite for a flight again. Just think about it. If you return with the kite in perfect condition, it seems that you bring disasters back home, doesn't it?

David: That makes sense. So, after you finish flying kites, you have to take off the paper, or you'll have bad luck. I'll keep that in mind. Now let's give it a try and see if our kite can rise high in the sky to bring us good luck.

Xiaolong: I'm sure it will!

佩香囊

> 小龙和大卫放完风筝,来到公园的后门。

大　卫:小龙,苏州的端午节习俗还有什么?

小　龙:最有特色的应该是苏州香囊。你看,不少人的背包上、手机上都挂着香囊呢。

大　卫:那是香囊呀,我还以为是个漂亮的装饰品呢。

小　龙:你说的也没错,不过它的作用可不仅是装饰。

大　卫:还有什么作用呢?

小　龙:还有驱虫防疫的功效。前面门口有个纪念品商店,应该会卖香囊。我们去看看,怎么样?

> 小龙和大卫进了商店。

大　卫:哇,这里的香囊真多啊。有圆的、方的,还有三角形的。有各种颜色和造型,好丰富呀。小龙,你

大 卫: 看，这个像只小粽子。

小 龙: 是的。你再闻闻。

大 卫: 有很特别的香味，很提神。

小 龙: 不同香囊里装的东西不一样，一般有雄黄、艾草等香料。

大 卫: 我知道，雄黄是一种中药材。

小 龙: 是的，很多香料都是中药材。端午节佩戴香囊不仅

佩香囊　Wearing Sachets

是一种装饰，也是利用这些香料的药性驱虫防病、提神醒脑。

大　卫：香囊这么有用，我得好好挑一个。我喜欢这两个香囊，一个金光闪闪，一个做工精细。

小　龙：香囊虽然各地都有，但说到做工精细，要数我们苏州特色的刺绣香囊，款式精美，小巧可爱，用的是苏州的丝绸和棉布。

大　卫：确实很不错。你看，那边还有老虎造型的香囊呢。

小　龙：那是苏州的一种传统香囊，叫"虎头香囊"。

大　卫：就像画额写"王"字一样，香囊做成虎头的模样也是为了辟邪，对吧？

小　龙：理解正确。

大　卫：小龙，我要买两个香囊，我们一人一个。谢谢你带我端午四地游。祝你端午快乐！

小　龙：谢谢！不过，我们一般不说"端午快乐"，而说"端午安康"，因为端午的习俗大多是为了辟邪防病。

大　卫：哦哦，明白了。端午安康！

小　龙：谢谢。也祝你端午安康！

Wearing Sachets

> Xiaolong and David headed to the back gate of the park after flying the kite.

David: Xiaolong, are there any other special Duanwu customs in Suzhou?

Xiaolong: I'd say the most distinctive one is wearing Suzhou sachets. As you can see, many people tie sachets to their backpacks and cell phones.

David: So they're sachets! I thought they were just pretty accessories.

Xiaolong: You're not mistaken. But sachets aren't only for decoration.

David: What else are they used for?

Xiaolong: They could be helpful in repelling insects and preventing disease. There's a souvenir shop ahead, next to the park entrance. They should have sachets. Let's go and take a look, shall we?

> The two entered the shop.

David: Wow, look at all these sachets! So many colours and shapes. There are plenty for us to choose: round ones, square ones, and even triangle-shaped ones. Look, Xiaolong. This one is like a little *zongzi*.

Xiaolong: Yes. Take one and smell it.

David: It has a particular smell, quite refreshing.

Xiaolong: Sachets are filled with different fragrant materials. They usually contain realgar, mugwort and others.

David: I know the first one. Realgar is used in traditional Chinese medicine.

Xiaolong: You're quite right. Many of those fragrant materials serve as ingredients in traditional Chinese medicine. People don't wear sachets only for decoration. Given the medicinal properties of the fillings, sachets can be effective in repelling insects, preventing diseases, as well as relaxing and refreshing the mind.

David: I didn't know they were so useful. Now I have to get myself one. I like these two. One shines with a golden colour, and the other is finely crafted.

Xiaolong: You can find sachets almost everywhere in China, but when it comes to workmanship, the intricately embroidered sachets made in Suzhou are second to none. They're made of local silk and cotton, tiny, exquisite, and lovely.

David: Indeed, they are excellent. Aha! Over there! They even have tiger-shaped sachets.

Xiaolong: That's a traditional kind of sachet in Suzhou, also known as the tiger head sachet. It's shaped like a tiger's head to keep evils at bay.

David: Oh, I know. Just like painting the character "王" on children's foreheads to protect them, tiger head sachets can help people stay safe from evils and misfortunes, right?

Xiaolong: Absolutely right.

David: Let me buy a sachet for each of us. Xiaolong, thank you for your company on this Duanwu trip. I enjoyed visiting all those places. And I want to wish you a happy Duanwu Festival!

Xiaolong: Thanks! Just a little reminder. Usually we don't say "Wish you a happy Duanwu Festival". Since most of the Duanwu customs are meant to ward off evils and prevent diseases, we actually say "Wish you a safe and healthy Duanwu Festival".

David: Oh, I see. Then, may you have a safe and healthy Duanwu Festival!

Xiaolong: Thanks, David. Likewise, I wish you a safe and sound Duanwu Festival!

挂菖蒲　插艾草

> 逛完公园之后，小龙和大卫来到苏州老城区。

大　卫：小龙，我特别喜欢苏州老城区。这里的房子和街道都很有特色。

小　龙：是的。你注意到家家户户的大门上挂着什么东西吗？

大　卫：正想问你呢。很多大门上挂着一束长长的叶子，这也是端午习俗吗？

小　龙：你说对了。那些长长的叶子是菖蒲，这个端午习俗叫"挂菖蒲"。

大　卫：这种叶子好像以前在哪里见过。

小　龙：有可能。菖蒲是一种水生植物，南方的池塘边和水渠里很常见。叶子能长到1米多高。你看，菖蒲叶子笔直，叶片顶端尖尖的，看起来像什么？

大　卫：像一把剑？

小　龙：没错！菖蒲也叫蒲剑、水剑，就是因为它的形状像把剑。民间把它看作斩妖除魔的象征，挂菖蒲是为了辟邪保平安。

大　卫：嗯，很有想象力。

小　龙：而且，菖蒲叶含有挥发性的香油，会散发一种特殊香味。端午节挂上它，真的能驱赶蚊虫，净化空气。

大　卫：这么说，挂菖蒲还挺有科学道理呢。

小　龙：是啊，菖蒲的作用可不止这个，它也是一种中药材。

大　卫：你是说它也可以治病吗？

小　龙：对。菖蒲的茎、叶、花都可以入药，能化痰、健胃。有些地方还用它酿酒，端午节时喝菖蒲酒。菖蒲外形很美，它象征正直的品格，所以自古就受文人喜爱。

大　卫：那我回去也要挂菖蒲。

小　龙：别急，端午节我们还在门上插艾草。很多人家既挂菖蒲，又插艾草。你看，这种细长的、叶子绒绒的草就是艾草。古代，人们还把艾草扎成人形或者虎

挂菖蒲 插艾草 Hanging Sweet Flags and Mugwort 139

挂菖蒲 Hanging Sweet Flags

插艾草 Hanging Mugwort

形,叫作"艾人"或"艾虎",可以挂在门上或者佩戴在身上。

大 卫:艾草有什么特别的用处?

小 龙:艾草的用处可多了。它有一种很浓烈的特殊香气,是天然的驱虫剂。过去在乡下,要是夏季晚上在院子里纳凉,人们经常会点着干艾草驱蚊子,特别有效。端午节家家户户插艾草,主要是为了驱赶蚊子和苍蝇等害虫。

大 卫:原来如此。艾草还有什么其他用处呢?

小 龙:有啊。艾草还是民间常见的药用植物,民间有"家有三年艾,郎中不用来"的谚语。

大 卫:这句话说的是什么意思?

小 龙:"郎中"在古汉语中指医生。这句话是说家里要是存有三年以上的艾草,就不用上医院看病了。端午节我们会用它泡水沐浴,能消毒止痒、驱邪保健。

大 卫:就和沐兰汤一样,是吗?

小 龙:是的,一样的功效。作为中药,它有止血、消炎和止咳的功效。对了,你知道艾灸吗?

大 卫:嗯,听说过,好像是中医里的一种治疗方法,但不知道具体是什么。

小　　龙：艾灸是中医的一种特殊治疗方法。首先要把艾叶晾干，然后碾碎成绒，再用纸把艾绒压紧，卷起来制成艾条。治病的时候点燃艾条，燃烧产生的热量刺激人体穴位或特定部位，可以疏通经络，防病保健。

大　　卫：这么神奇吗？有机会我也去体验一下。

小　　龙：还有呢，艾草还能做成糕点。现在人们已经用艾草开发出两百多种日常生活用品了，还有艾草咖啡呢。

大　　卫：哇，还有什么是艾草不能做的！你知道吗？我来苏州上学，特别喜欢这里的点心。不过还没吃过艾草做的点心呢。它可以做成什么糕点呢？

小　　龙：每个地方的做法不一样，大多是把艾草的汁液拌进米粉，做成各式糕点，比如艾草青团。艾草汁液做出的点心颜色翠绿，还有淡淡的艾草清香，大家都很喜欢吃。

大　　卫：嗯，我一定要尝尝。

小　　龙：好啊，我知道学校附近有家点心店，端午前后会卖青团。等回到学校，我们买一些尝尝。对了，端午的时候，我们还会在糕点上点缀五毒图案，那样的话,吃掉糕点就意味着消灭五毒啦。

大　卫:好的,那我们就多买几种,吃糕点,灭五毒。

Hanging Sweet Flags and Mugwort

After their walk in the park, Xiaolong and David arrived at the Old Town of Suzhou.

David: This is one of my favourite places in Suzhou. The houses and streets here are unique.

Xiaolong: Yes, indeed. Have you noticed that every house has something hanging on the front door?

David: I was just about to ask. What are those long leaves? Is this a Duanwu custom as well?

Xiaolong: You're right. This is the tradition of hanging sweet flags on the front door.

David: I think I've seen this plant somewhere before.

Xiaolong: I'm sure you have. Sweet flag is an aquatic plant. It's common in southern China and grows by ponds and streams. The leaves can reach over one-metre long. Look at the straight leaves and the pointed tips. What do they look like?

David: A sword?

Xiaolong: Bingo! That's why sweet flag is also known as sweet flag sword or water sword in Chinese. It's seen as a symbol to drive away evil spirits, and hung outside to ward off evils and bring safety to people.

David: Well, that's very imaginative.

Xiaolong: Very much so. Besides, sweet flag produces an aromatic oil, giving off a particular fragrance. If you hang it on the door during the Duanwu Festival, it helps with keeping insects away and the air clear and clean.

David: So, there's a scientific reason for hanging it.

Xiaolong: Absolutely. But there're other uses as it's also a medicinal herb.

David: You're saying it can cure diseases?

Xiaolong: Yes. The stems, leaves, and flowers can all be used as medicine to cure coughs and promote stomach health.

People also make wine with it to drink during the Duanwu Festival. Moreover, ancient scholars were fond of sweet flags and viewed the beautiful plant as a symbol of integrity.

David: I'll hang sweet flags, too, when I get back.

Xiaolong: And that's not all. We also hang mugwort on the front door during the Duanwu Festival. Many people hang both sweet flags and mugwort. The long and thin plant with fluffy leaves is mugwort. People in ancient times would weave it into a human shape or a tiger shape, called mugwort man or mugwort tiger. These mugwort fugurines could be hung on the front door or worn as an accessory.

David: What can we do with mugwort?

Xiaolong: It can do a lot. It has a strong scent as well, so it makes for a perfect insect repellent. In old times, when people in the rural area were out in the yard enjoying the cool summer night breeze, they would burn dried mugwort as it was very effective in keeping mosquitoes away. Nowadays, people hang mugwort during the Duanwu Festival mainly to drive away mosquitoes, flies, and other harmful insects.

David: I see. Is there anything else you can do with it?

Xiaolong: Well, of course. Mugwort is also a commonly used herbal medicine. A folk saying goes, "If you have mugwort stored for three years at your home, *langzhong* (郎中) won't show his face."

David: What does it mean?

Xiaolong: *Langzhong* means doctor in ancient Chinese. This saying means that if you pick mugwort and store it for three years in your house, you won't have to go to see a doctor. During the Duanwu Festival, we bath in mugwort water because it kills germs, stops itch, drives away evils, and keeps us safe.

David: It's similar to having herbal baths, isn't it?

Xiaolong: Yes, they have the same effect. Mugwort is also used to stop bleeding and cure inflammation and coughs. By the way, do you know moxibustion?

David: I've heard of it. I know it's a part of traditional Chinese medicine. Besides that, I don't know what exactly it is.

Xiaolong: You're right. Moxibustion is a special therapy in traditional Chinese medicine and involves several steps. First, dry the mugwort leaves and then grind them into fine fluff. Second, roll them up into sticks with paper. Finally, use the stick as a means of treatment. You have to burn the mugwort stick close to the skin, and the heat produced will stimulate certain acupoints or parts of the body. Moxibustion therapy can improve the flow of energy in the body, prevent diseases, and improve health.

David: Sounds magic! I'll give it a try if I ever get the chance.

Xiaolong: And there's more. People have developed more than two hundred products with mugwort for everyday use. It can be used as an ingredient to make pastry. There is even mugwort coffee.

David: Wow, is there anything you can't do with it? You know one thing that I really enjoy about studying in Suzhou is that I love the local desserts. But I haven't tried mugwort pastry yet. What kind of pastries can you make with mugwort?

Xiaolong: The recipe is different from place to place. Usually, people mix mugwort juice with rice flour and knead it into different types of pastries, like mugwort *qingtuan* (青团), which is a kind of sticky rice snack. The pastries are emerald green and have a light pleasant smell of mugwort.

David: My mouth is already watering. I want to try it.

Xiaolong: I know a shop near our school that sells *qingtuan* around the Duanwu Festival. Let's buy some on our way back. Some of the pastries are decorated with images of the five poisonous creatures. Eating them symbolises getting rid of them.

David: Okay. Let's eat some pastries and get rid of the poisonous creatures.

射柳　打马球

> 小龙和大卫回到学校。他们路过点心店，买了几种青团。两人来到小龙宿舍，一起喝茶吃青团。

大　卫：小龙，这个青团不错，颜色好看，绿绿的，也挺好吃。

小　龙：嗯，青团是江南地区的传统小吃，古代清明时节人们还用它来祭祖，现在是大家春游必带的美食了。

大　卫：中国北方应该没有青团吧。中国南北方的端午习俗一样吗？

小　龙：不完全一样。吃粽子、避五毒、斗百草、放风筝是南北方都有的习俗，划龙舟、闻雄黄酒是南方习俗，过去北方最热闹的端午习俗是射柳和打马球，现在好像已经完全消失了。

大　卫：真可惜，我们看不到了。

小　龙：确实。不过，我知道有个地方可以了解这两个习俗，苏州博物馆正好有个关于端午风俗的展览。我们找个时间去看看，好不好？

大　卫：太好了，那明天下午我们一起去吧。

> 第二天下午，小龙和大卫来到苏州博物馆，他们找到了端午特展与射柳和马球相关的内容。

小　龙：大卫，快来看。说明牌上说，射柳和马球都是北方的端午习俗，人们会在端午节清晨举行骑马射柳的活动。哦，先要将柳树干的中上部削去一段青皮，露出白色，依次插在马球场上作为靶心。然后，参赛者骑马拉弓，射向柳树削白的地方，射断柳树后，还得骑着马用手接住断柳。

大　卫：这个可不容易啊。小龙，你看，这还有张图，上面的骑手正把箭头对准柳树，拉弓射箭呢。

小　龙：是的，但射柳的概念更广泛，不一定都是射柳树。你再往下看就知道了。

大　卫：是吗？

小　龙：你看，这里介绍了射柳的起源。早在2500多年前的春秋战国时期，孔子的"六礼"中就有"射礼"，射礼曾是中国传统文化中修身的一项内容。端午民俗中的射箭起初是中国古代北方游牧民族的一项活动，可以追溯到魏晋南北朝时期，后来慢慢成为北方地区的习俗。

大　卫：骑马射箭确实是游牧民族擅长的活动。

小　龙：没错。大卫你看，介绍上说，唐宋时期，射柳在民间很普遍。集会时有比赛和表演，分为步射和骑射，有固定箭靶，也有流动箭靶，有人甚至能在马上用各种不同的动作射中靶呢。

大　卫：那一定特别惊险刺激。

小　龙：那是肯定的。还有，这里说北宋时期就明确规定，每年农历的三月初三和五月初五这两天，举行射柳比赛。不过主要限于军队内部，目的是提升军队的战斗力。

> 大卫认真地看着展览介绍，听小龙小声解释图片上面的文字。

大　卫：小龙你看，好像后面各个朝代都有这个活动呀。

小　龙：对，介绍得很详细。元朝时期，射柳活动在贵族生活中也很流行。不过，大卫你看，到了明朝，射柳的形式就有变化了。

射柳　Shooting Arrows at Willow Branches

大　卫：有什么变化呢？

小　龙：到了明朝永乐年间，射柳活动的形式就变成将鸽子放在葫芦里，然后将葫芦高挂在柳树上，用箭射中葫芦后鸽子飞出，最后以鸽子飞的高度来判定胜负。

大　卫：这个更有趣。哦，我明白了。难怪你刚才说射柳不

射柳 打马球 Shooting Arrows at Willow Branches and Playing Polo 153

一定就是射柳树呢。

小　龙：是啊。大卫，你再看这幅图。这是清朝时人们射柳的情形。但到了100多年前，端午节已经基本看不到射柳活动了。

大　卫：好遗憾呀。要不然，现在的端午节会更热闹，我们也能去学学射柳。

打马球　Playing Polo

小　龙：没错。大卫，其实还有一项北方端午民俗也消失了，也很可惜。

大　卫：你说的是打马球吧。

小　龙：是的。大卫，你来看，这里画的正是古人打马球的场景。

大　卫：画得很生动呢。小龙，你看这些人手里挥舞着球杆争抢击球。这看上去和现代马球运动也差不多。

小　龙：打马球的民俗我不是很了解，我们请讲解员来讲解一下吧。

> 小龙和大卫向讲解员了解打马球的细节。

讲解员：两位好，我来给你们介绍下打马球的端午民俗。请看这里，这幅画画的是唐代打马球的场景。打马球一般有20多人参与，分成两队，从马上用球杖击球，打入对方球门。这在当时是一种很时髦的游戏活动。

小　龙：这么说，早在唐朝，我们就有马球运动了。

讲解员：是的。马球出现的时间一直有争议，有一种说法是最早出现在汉朝。不过，马球盛行于唐、宋、元三个朝代。唐朝打马球风行一时，但用途不一样。王公贵族打马球是娱乐，军队打马球是军事训练。而且，当时马球比赛还成为一种交际手段。

小　龙：交际手段？

讲解员：是的。故宫博物院藏有一幅古画，描绘了唐朝时期一场马球比赛的场面。其实，马球和射柳一样，都是从军事训练活动演变而来的。

大　卫：那打马球和端午节有什么关系呢？

讲解员：有关系呀，打马球也是北方端午节的重要民俗活动。事实上，元朝和明朝，北方地区都保留端午节打马球的风俗。马球是在清朝完全绝迹的，这和清朝禁止百姓习武、养马有关。所以，后来这两项北方端午习俗就慢慢消失了。

大　卫：原来是这样。谢谢您的讲解。

讲解员：不客气！祝你们参观愉快。

大　卫：小龙，原来射柳、打马球的历史还很悠久呢。不过现在只能在博物馆里见到了。

小　龙：这两项端午民俗也算是非物质文化遗产了。以后要能恢复就好了，大家应该也会有兴趣参与吧。

大　卫：你说得对。要是以后恢复这些民俗活动，我一定也来试试。

小　龙：那你就真成了"中国通"啦。

大　卫：那当然，我回国以后也要跟家人朋友讲讲中国端午节有趣的民俗，告诉他们中国人为什么过端午。他们一定想不到，端午节其实是中国古代的"卫生防疫节"。

Shooting Arrows at Willow Branches and Playing Polo

> On their way back to the university, Xiaolong and David stopped by a pastry shop and bought some *qingtuan*. They went to Xiaolong's dormitory to have a Chinese afternoon tea.

David: This *qingtuan* is nice. I like the colour, a pretty shade of green. It tastes good, too.

Xiaolong: It does. *Qingtuan* is a traditional snack in the lower reaches of the Yangtze River. It served as an offering during the Qingming Festival when people held ceremonies to worship their ancestors. Now it has become a must-have snack for spring outings.

David: I suppose people don't eat *qingtuan* in northern China? Are the Duanwu customs the same in northern and southern China?

Xiaolong: For one thing, the customs aren't entirely the same. Eating *zongzi*, warding off *wudu*, matching herbs, and flying kites are common to both northern and southern China. Rowing dragon boats and sniffing realgar wine are specific to southern China. As for the northern part of the country, the most entertaining Duanwu customs were shooting arrows at willow branches and playing polo. But that was in the past. I don't think people perform them anymore.

David: It's a pity that we can't see them.

Xiaolong: I know. But I've heard of a place for us to learn more about those practices. The Suzhou Museum is currently holding an exhibition about Duanwu customs. Shall we stop by sometime?

David: Sounds great. Let's go and check it out tomorrow afternoon.

> The next afternoon, Xiaolong and David arrived at the Suzhou Museum and visited the exhibition on the two Duanwu customs in northern China.

Xiaolong: David, look at the label. It says that both shooting

射柳 打马球 Shooting Arrows at Willow Branches and Playing Polo 159

arrows at willow branches and playing polo were Duanwu customs specific to northern China. During the Duanwu Festival, people usually gather in the early morning for an annual event of willow shooting. Oh, it also says here that they first cut off the bark at the upper middle part of a willow trunk and expose the inner part. Then, they line up the willow trunks in the polo field with the bare patches serving as bull's eyes. The players would then shoot the patches with arrows from horseback. As soon as the trunk splits off, they have to speed up the horse and catch the falling part before it hits the ground.

Xiaolong: It seems very difficult. Hey, Xiaolong, look at this picture. The horseman is drawing his bow and aiming at a willow tree.

Xiaolong: Actually, they also shot at other targets besides willow branches. You'll soon see it for yourself.

David: Is that so?

Xiaolong: Here's an interpretation of the origin of the custom. Back in the Spring and Autumn Period and the

Warring States Period, more than 2,500 years ago, archery was one of the "Six Rituals" proposed by Confucius. It was an important part of self-cultivation in traditional culture. Shooting as a Duanwu custom originated from an archery activity of the northern nomadic people in ancient China. It can be traced back to the Western and Eastern Jin dynasties and the Northern and Southern dynasties. Later, it developed into a custom in the north.

David: Well, nomadic people are truly skilled at horseback riding and archery.

Xiaolong: You're quite right. According to the description, in the Tang and Song dynasties, shooting arrows at willow branches was quite popular. During gatherings, people would organize shooting competitions and performances. The activities included archery and mounted archery, shooting both at stationary and moving targets. Some players could even hit the target while performing different poses on horseback.

David: I'm sure that it must have been very thrilling.

射柳 打马球 Shooting Arrows at Willow Branches and Playing Polo

Xiaolong: Certainly! Shooting arrows at willow branches was performed annually on the third day of the third lunar month and the fifth day of the fifth lunar month in the Northern Song Dynasty. But this practice was mainly organised within the army and meant to increase its combat power.

> David was all eyes and ears, checking the exhibition's presentations and listening to Xiaolong read the interpretations in a low voice.

David: Xiaolong, it seems this practice continued in the following dynasties as well.

Xiaolong: Yes. It's explained here in detail. In the Yuan Dynasty, shooting arrows at willow branches became a fun activity among the nobles. But as you can see, in the Ming Dynasty the way it was played changed.

David: What happened?

Xiaolong: During the reign of Emperor Yongle of the Ming Dynasty, shooting arrows at willow branches evolved into a contest. A gourd with a pigeon placed inside was hung high up in a tree. The archers were supposed to shoot the gourd to release the pigeon. The archer won the game when his pigeon flied the highest.

David: This sounds more interesting. Now I understand why you said they shot at targets other than willow branches.

Xiaolong: Exactly. Look at this picture. It illustrates how they performed shooting arrows at willow branches in the Qing Dynasty. But this practice was no longer a part of the Duanwu celebrations about 100 years ago.

David: What a pity! The Duanwu Festival would be even more exciting if people still did this activity now, and we could learn it.

Xiaolong: I agree. Unfortunately, it's not the only Duanwu custom in northern China that has disappeared.

David: Are you talking about polo?

Xiaolong: Yes. Look at this picture. It's a painting of ancient Chinese playing a game of polo.

David: It's very vivid. Xiaolong, those five people are waving their sticks to kick the ball. It doesn't seem too different from modern polo.

Xiaolong: Well, I'm not very familiar with this custom. We should ask a guide to explain it to us.

> Xiaolong and David found a guide to tell them more about the tradition of playing polo.

Guide: Hello! Playing polo is a sport with a long history in China. Look at this picture. It's a scene of polo playing in the Tang Dynasty. This game was played by about 20 people who were divided into two teams. The players used a mallet to hit the ball, and victory went to those who hit the ball through the opponents' goal. It was a popular sport then.

Xiaolong: So, playing polo could date back to the Tang Dynasty.

Guide: Yes. There are always different views on when polo appeared. Some argue that it started in the Han Dynasty. What's known for sure is that the sport was very popular in the Tang, Song, and Yuan dynasties. In the Tang Dynasty, for example, it was in fashion and served different purposes. The nobles played it for entertainment, and the soldiers played it for military training. There was even polo communication strategy.

Xiaolong: What do you mean by polo communication strategy?

Guide: The Palace Museum in Beijing houses a painting that depicts a polo match during the Tang Dynasty. Actually, both playing polo and shooting arrows at willow branches developed from military training.

David: Is there any connection between polo playing and the Duanwu Festival?

Guide: Yes. Playing polo was an important Duanwu custom in northern China and was preserved until the Yuan and Ming dynasties. But it died out in the Qing Dynasty, when the rulers banned practicing martial arts and raising horses. That's why shooting arrows at willow branches and playing polo gradually disappeared.

David: I see. Thank you for your interpretation!

Guide: My pleasure. Enjoy your visit!

David: Xiaolong, I didn't know shooting arrows at willow branches and playing polo had such a long history. It's a pity we can only find them in a museum now.

Xiaolong: Yes. The two Duanwu customs are part of the Chinese intangible cultural heritage. I hope one day they could be revived. I'm sure people would like to participate in those activities.

David: Of course. If those practices are ever resumed, I'll definitely give it a try.

Xiaolong: In that case, you'd become a real China hand.

David: You can be sure of that. I'll tell my family and friends about the fascinating Duanwu customs when I'm back home. I'll describe to them how Chinese people celebrate the Duanwu Festival. They would probably have never guessed that the Duanwu Festival was a festival for good health and epidemic prevention in ancient China.

结束语

通过端午假期的游览和体验,小龙和大卫对中国端午节有了全新认识。端午节是中华民族重要的传统节日,它记录着中国人多彩的社会生活和民间习俗,积淀了博大精深的中国文化。各地的端午习俗虽因地域不同而略有差异,但都寄托了人们迎祥纳福、辟邪除灾的美好愿望。端午期间人们用来祛病防疫的各种传统习俗蕴含着中国古人的生活智慧,值得代代相传。

Summary

The experiential travel Xiaolong and David had during the Duanwu holiday offered them a new understanding of the traditional Chinese festival. As one of the important traditional Chinese festivals, Duanwu, or the Dragon Boat Festival, stands as a historical record of the vibrant social life and activities of Chinese people, an indispensable part of the great Chinese civilization. Even though its customs vary slightly from one region to another, they are all means for people to ask for blessings, to ward off evils, and to avoid disasters. Those practices that people carry out during Duanwu to prevent diseases are infused with ancient Chinese wisdom and should be passed on to the future generations.

中国历史纪年简表
A Brief Chronology of Chinese History

夏	Xia Dynasty			c. 2070—1600 B.C.
商	Shang Dynasty			1600—1046 B.C.
周	Zhou Dynasty	西周	Western Zhou Dynasty	1046—771 B.C.
		东周	Eastern Zhou Dynasty	770—256 B.C.
		春秋	Spring and Autumn Period	770—476 B.C.
		战国	Warring States Period	475—221 B.C.
秦	Qin Dynasty			221—206 B.C.
汉	Han Dynasty	西汉	Western Han Dynasty	206 B.C.—25
		东汉	Eastern Han Dynasty	25—220
三国	Three Kingdoms			220—280
西晋	Western Jin Dynasty			265—317
东晋	Eastern Jin Dynasty			317—420
南北朝	Northern and Southern Dynasties	南朝	Southern Dynasties	420—589
		北朝	Northern Dynasties	386—581
隋	Sui Dynasty			581—618
唐	Tang Dynasty			618—907
五代	Five Dynasties			907—960
宋	Song Dynasty			960—1279
辽	Liao Dynasty			907—1125
金	Jin Dynasty			1115—1234
元	Yuan Dynasty			1206—1368
明	Ming Dynasty			1368—1644
清	Qing Dynasty			1616—1911
中华民国	Republic of China			1912—1949
中华人民共和国	People's Republic of China			1949—

图书在版编目(CIP)数据

端午节:汉英对照 / 魏向清,恽如强主编. —— 南京:南京大学出版社,2024.8
(中国世界级非遗文化悦读系列 / 魏向清,刘润泽主编. 寻语识遗)
ISBN 978-7-305-26447-4

Ⅰ.①端… Ⅱ.①魏…②恽… Ⅲ.①端午节-介绍-中国-汉、英 Ⅳ.① K892.18

中国版本图书馆 CIP 数据核字(2022)第 246063 号

出版发行	南京大学出版社		
社　　址	南京市汉口路 22 号	邮　编	210093

丛 书 名　中国世界级非遗文化悦读系列·寻语识遗
丛书主编　魏向清　刘润泽
书　　名　**端午节:汉英对照**
　　　　　　DUANWUJIE: HANYING DUIZHAO
主　　编　魏向清　恽如强
责任编辑　张淑文　　　编辑热线　(025)83592401

照　　排	南京新华丰制版有限公司
印　　刷	南京凯德印刷有限公司
开　　本	880mm×1230mm　1/32 开　印张 5.875　字数 122 千
版　　次	2024 年 8 月第 1 版　2024 年 8 月第 1 次印刷

ISBN 978-7-305-26447-4
定　　价　69.00 元

网址:http://www.njupco.com
官方微博:http://weibo.com/njupco
官方微信号:njupress
销售咨询热线:(025)83594756

* 版权所有,侵权必究

* 凡购买南大版图书,如有印装质量问题,请与所购图书销售部门联系调换